I'm Good

I'm Good

Overcoming the Promise of Pain

ASIA MONAE CARLTON

Copyright © 2021 by Asia Monae Carlton
All rights reserved. No part of this publication may be reproduced, scanned, uploaded, stored in a retrieval system, or transmitted, in any form or by any means, electronic, mechanical, photocopying, recording, or otherwise, without the prior written permission of the publisher.

Scriptures marked AMP are
taken from the Amplified version, public domain.
ISBN: 979-8-218-02699-8
Publisher: Asia Monae Carlton
Publisher Consultant:
Sophisticated Press

Book Design
Sophisticated Press
Photographer

Asia Monae Carlton

Manufactured in the United States of America

"Come to Me, all who are weary and heavily burdened [by religious rituals that provide no peace], and I will give you rest [refreshing your souls with salvation]. Take My yoke upon you and learn from Me [following my disciples], for I am gentle and humble in heart, and **YOU WILL FIND REST** (renewal, blessed quiet) **FOR YOUR SOULS.** For My yoke is easy [to bear] and My burden is light."

-Matthew 11: 28-30 AMP

DEDICATION

Holy Spirit, thank you! Thank you for leading and guiding me. Thank you for your instruction and protection. Jesus, thank you! Thank you for taking one for the team. Thank you for your example and your teachings. Thank you for your sacrifice. Father God, my love, my King, thank you for creating me. Thank you for strategically placing gifts & talents in me. Thank you for the ability to produce and multiply. May all that I do bring glory to Your name. Thank you for loving me in every season, even in those that I didn't love myself. Thank you for writing my story, our story to share. Thank you for being You, for always keeping your hand on me, for patience and process. Thank you for removing the element of performance and replacing it with praise. I bless your holy name. Thank you for setting me apart. Thank you for my inheritance. Thank you for your children, oh God. May we all continue to be transformed by the renewing of our minds, the words of our testimonies, and your unfailing love. Thank you for your peace in every storm of life. I thank you that with you, we really can say, "I'm Good".

TO THE READER

My prayer is that this text blesses you in a way that transforms your life. Each one of these chapters are catered to an area of struggle that causes pain. Know that there is a breakthrough on the other side of every struggle. Pain is not everlasting. Joy comes in the morning.

Table of Contents

Introduction 1

Let's Get Down to the Bottom of This 3

Childhood Trauma (Flawed Foundation) 5

I Get It From My Momma (Generational Curses) 10

It's Just The Way I Am (False Identity) 16

Only God Can Judge Me (Yet I Judge Myself) 23

Don't Try Me (Living with Offense) 27

You Owe Me An Apology (Bitterness) 31

Do You Love Me (Searching for Love) 39

It's All About Me (Selfishness) 45

I'm Grown (More Growing to Do) 54

I Like It Like That (Refusing Change) 59

If God Is Real (Dealing with Loss) 64

I'm Taking It To My Grave (The secret about secrets) 68

I Can Breathe Again (Giving it All to God) 72

Introduction

"I'm Good". How many of us have heard this or used this statement when someone asks, "How are you"? This two-word statement is one of the biggest and most common lies that we tell ourselves and others. Have you ever considered why it's our default? I have. We're often taught to put a smile on our face, put our best foot forward, or not to concern anyone with our personal affairs. Maybe we've been convinced that nobody cares about our pain or struggles. Sometimes we can believe it so much that we believe the lie causing us to neglect those parts of us that desperately need attention.

You owe it to yourself, your family, your supporters, your destiny, and EVERYTHING connected to you, to make sure you tend to everything that has the potential to hold you back from your God-given destiny, regardless of the hurt. Today is the day that we stop pacifying our pain. Today is the day we stop fearing what facing that pain may mean. Today we step into our God-given power and bring our thoughts, emotions, and feelings into submission. Today we stop telling the lie, "I'm Good".

Now before you get scared and close this book, There are some questions to consider:

1. Do I deserve better than my current circumstances?

2. Do I want to change?

3. Am I willing to do the work necessary for progress?

4. Am I ready to say goodbye to the things that no longer serve me and make room for things that do?

If you answered yes to any of the following questions, then I invite you to continue reading, as I expose my life, love, losses, lessons and level up process! In case you were unsure, Yes! You do deserve better, regardless of what you have done or what you have been through. Yes! You do want to change. Stagnation is death. Yes! You are willing to do the necessary work for progress because you know that you deserve better than your current circumstances. Yes! You are ready to say goodbye to things that no longer serve you and make room for things that do because you are WORTH IT!

So let's do it together.

CHAPTER 1

Let's Get Down to the Bottom of This

I grew up in the church, sitting next to my Mom Mom, Deaconess Barbara Johnson. We worshiped in song and danced together. I can remember being so small and not completely understanding what or who the Holy Spirit was, but feeling His presence. I can remember sitting in the adult church listening and surprisingly comprehending the Word. One concept that I *thought* I understood immediately was pain & sacrifice. I found the commonalities between all of the Bible's trailblazers. They all endured pain and struggle and *that* frightened me. I didn't want to have to endure turmoil just to be with my Lord. I remember my mom telling me that one time I came to her crying and claiming that I wanted to die to be with Jesus because I loved Him so much. And it's true, I do love Him, but I was also terrified of Him.

I figured, Hey, God gave us an outline of what to do and what not to do in the Bible. If I just do the "right" thing and learn from the mistakes of others, I could use wisdom not to place myself on a path that would cause me hardship and pain. I was deathly afraid of pain. So much so, that I wanted to do EVERYTHING right. I wanted to have straight A's in school, be a good big sister, an obedient daughter, a sweet granddaughter and a representative of God. I know, that's quite an expectation for a 7-year- old, but that's what I desired. Later, I would learn that my yearning to be "right" and "good" would cause me to be unfairly judgmental and critical of my own shortcomings. In my adolescence, I couldn't understand the difference between knowledge, wisdom and understanding. I had the knowledge to know what was right and wrong. I had enough wisdom to know that if I did the wrong things, that unpleasant outcomes shortly followed. However, I did not understand that in order to truly please God, I would have to make some wrong turns, experience unpleasant outcomes, and endure pain in order to grow into the fullness of who He has called me to be.

CHAPTER 2

Childhood Trauma (Flawed Foundation)

It always amazes me when adults talk *loosely* in front of children. Kids are often exposed to *adult* content, unhealthy relationships and problematic habits. This isn't a judgment, but rather an observation. An observation I'm amazed by, because I'm amazed by what I remember from my own childhood. For example, I can remember there always being alcohol present and hearing arguments between adults where they are screaming and hollering and cussing. I can remember my mother singing her heart out to old Mary J. Blige and Teena Marie. I remember visiting my uncle in prison. I remember my first sexual encounter on the back of my Pre-K school bus. I remember Lady Tina holding my head in her hands, looking me in my eyes, and telling me that I'm special and that God has a purpose for my life. Yea, I remember a lot from my childhood and let me tell you, I had an amazing one. Interestingly enough, I experienced everything in my adult life that I was exposed to as a child.

I find that many adults, and especially young parents in their early and mid-twenties, don't realize what they are exposing their children to. I don't think they realize that everything a child experiences is a seed in their foundational makeup. (And I don't think they realize this, because most of us are trying to figure out who we are in our early twenties.) I'm not a mother yet, but I'm making it a personal mission to be intentional about letting God reveal and remove unhealthy patterns and habits from my life. This world does a great job with over-exposure, but learning starts at home for sure. Our modes of communication (or lack thereof), displays of love, sense of identity and pain management tactics are learned at home. Let's focus on dealing with pain for a moment, as we visit my childhood home.

I was raised by a strong, loving, beautiful, and sassy single mother. Her main support system consisted of her mother, stepfather, (Mom Mom & Pop Pop to me), grandmother, her best friend (my Godmother), and her Sister cousins Bridgette and Lisa. I wonder if my mom would agree that this was her main team, but this is how I saw it. I somewhat knew my father. I knew of him, but never *knew* him, you feel me? In my eyes, my Pop Pop was my father figure. When I wasn't at home with my mother, or at school, I could primarily be found in the care of my grandparents. Mom Mom & Pop Pop's house was my favorite place to be. At their house, I got to bake cakes with Mom Mom or watch Disney movies. Pop Pop was my best friend. He knew how to play! His imagination might have been bigger than mine. Pop Pop rant!

I was a Pop Pop's girl. This man would get on his hands and knees and chase me around the living room for what seemed like an eternity, while I would laugh and scream for Mom Mom to come and get the monster. We would watch Ichabod Crane, and he would test me on all the characters and encourage me to make the sounds of the animals in the forest. Or better yet, I would climb up in his lap while we watched his favorite westerns like The O.K. Coral, while we sang the theme song. He would give me "a sip" of his soda, just for me to return an empty can to him and run away laughing. He would come into my bedroom and kill the beetles when I called for him, and then sneak me cookies or pretzels though Mom Mom said it was time for bed. He let me help him build and fix things around the house. He even let me drive his tractor! He removed wasp stings from my head when I got stung outback on the swingset. He took me out on dates to my favorite fast-food restaurants and said," Fruitfly, this is only once in a while cuz this food is no good for you!" When my mom would try to come and get me, I would cry to stay with them, not because I didn't like home, but because I had a ball at Mom Mom's and Pop Pop's. Ok - Point is I LOVE that man, rest his soul.

I thought for a long time that I didn't need my father because I had my Pop Pop. Besides, it was normal in my city for children to be without their fathers. But not many had both their grandparents alive and involved like mine. That mindset was a seed of rejection, buried under the love of another man, one I would have to deal with later in my early twenties. Where were we? Oh yes, the thing we're looking for is pain. The first time I felt pain.

One time in school, I must have gotten above myself, so much to the point, I received a call home. I remember feeling betrayed by Mr. Harry, my choir director, and the man who introduced me to my love of music. I got a beatin' when I went home, just three licks. I was so sad. I laid there with my lil cheeks out, crying and thinking, I don't like this. Furthermore, I thought, my mommy was unhappy with me. I was sad, and had that same thought I had in church. If you're bad, you're gonna have pain waiting for you on the other side. I decided at that moment, not to misbehave anymore. I was going to be a good girl and unproblematic. The problem with being a "good girl", mistakes become the end of the world. I didn't like the pain inflicted on me, neither did I like the fact that it came from my mother. I became obsessed with "showing" my mom that I was a good girl to avoid more pain and disappointment, a habit I later repeated in my relationship with God.

When your children "fear" you, they tend to hide their shortcomings from you, which forfeits the opportunity for you to guide them through hardships at various stages. I think it's important to explain to your children why there are certain boundaries for them. I think that when a parent hits a child, it's more about the lack of patience that the parent has or their pride. If you ask a parent why they beat their kids you might get a response like, " They're bad,

They don't listen" or "They ain't gonna embarrass me". This is a dangerous seed to implant. Again, not a judgment, plenty of people got beatin's as children by their parents. It's a generational thing in African-American culture that stems from slavery. You teach your children "Obey me, or you gon' get this work." I'm a firm believer in discipline, but parents should think about the desired outcome. It's only so many times that you can strike a child until they get old enough to strike back, in the same ways slaves revolted against their masters. There has to be a distinction between plantations and parenthood. Parenthood is the first love relationship a child experiences. You teach your children how to love by how you love them. You teach your children how to speak in the way you speak to them. That's why it's so important to be intentional in the way you communicate with them. Let kids be kids, and allow them to learn. Guide them through their shortcomings, and create a safe haven for them to be vulnerable.

Parents, YOUR KIDS DO NOT COME OUT PERFECT. It is your duty to love them, teach them and mold them. I find that it's difficult for some parents to show love in a healthy way because they are still hurting from the pain of their own lives. Hurt people really do hurt people, even if it's unintentional. The intention may be to discipline for structure's thought maybe, "Well this is how I was raised," but just because it is so, does not mean it is right. Consider this, what affected you most in your childhood? Should children be taught to endure physical/mental pain from those who are supposed to love and protect them? What happens when the child is exposed to pain, but not taught how to deal with the pain? Everything is a seed.

I didn't get beatin's often. In fact, I can maybe count three times in my whole life. But I do know what was effective for me, PUNISHMENT. It was the worst. No Tv, no games, and going to bed early. I dreaded punishment and I think my mom knew it. The benefit of punishment was that it encouraged me to be obedient. Obedience is key. Obedience was for my benefit. Here's how. My mom made it very clear that she meant what she said. I was no stranger to the hard work she did to provide for my brother and I, and she was no stranger to letting me know that the things I enjoyed would be taken away if I wasn't obedient. The fact that I had access to TV and toys let me know that my mom wanted me to have an enjoyable life. She didn't want me to sit in my room bored. By that same token, if she said to clean up the toys or they would be thrown away, I got the clear message that if I wanted to enjoy my blessings, I had to be obedient to the one that provided them. God does the same thing. He provides all of our needs and plenty of our wants, some of which we are undeserving of. However, when He gives us instructions, He wants us to be obedient so that He can continue to bless us. He doesn't want to take the blessings away. He paid for them! But when we become disobedient, He will take those blessings away so we can sit in our quiet places and think about how we wish we would have been obedient. I thank my mom for putting me on punishment when she needed to get her message across. I learned to keep my room clean and gained an appreciation for organization. Obedience is a gift you can give to yourself. Obedience suggests, you have a choice! Choose wisely, because your obedience is in direct correlation with your success.

CHAPTER 3

I Get It From My Momma (Generational Curses)

The older I get, the more I realize how much I am like my mother; from our independence, to the tone of our voices, or love of cooking and hosting, our laugh is even the same. I was in a four-year relationship from 19-23. After some much-needed reflection, I realized that our similarities were greater than I thought. We were alike in our communication methods, pain management tactics, lack of patience and feelings of being unappreciated. Much like my mother, I had to ALWAYS have the last word. My sense of pride was so intense, that my ex actually told me early on that it would be the thing to ruin us, and in some regard, he was right. It definitely played a huge part in our demise. I have been blessed with the gift of the lip. One which in the past, I have tainted by turning my gift into a tool of manipulation. Mix pride, with hyper-independence, feelings of being unappreciated plus a mouth almighty and "My way or the highway" mindset, and you end up with a dangerous complex. My mindset was, that if you really love me, you will do whatever it takes to please me and make me happy. It sounds so immature and that's because it is. In my relationship, I found myself "testing" my partner, I mean really making him jump through hoops to prove his love and my worthiness of that love. This was super dangerous for both of us. A person will never make you happy all of the time. Any good relationship will test you in positive ways and challenge you to become a better version of yourself. A healthy relationship will open you up to your insecurities in a loving way and cause you to start tackling them. A loving relationship will push you towards becoming an enhanced version of yourself rather than stroke your ego and tell you whatever you want to hear to maintain peace and happiness. I desire a relationship that constantly challenges me in a healthy, loving way. That is how one obtains true growth and shaping.

I didn't understand that then. No, I wanted him to pass every unfair test that I set up, and when he didn't pass with flying colors, I was crushed. I felt as if he didn't really love me. My confidence started to fade and I began to wonder why I wasn't "good enough". Eventually, he became sick of my antics and I don't blame him. I mean I was really a piece of work. Arguing with me was like going to court with Olivia Pope, but a savage version. My manipulation skills were impeccable. I could make you leave an argument unsure of where you stood, because of how passionately I would force my point of view down your throat. And then once I made you feel terrible, I'd lift your spirit with sexual therapy. I know y'all, I told you I was a piece of work. It was so bad because I could see him really trying to understand me, but I was struggling to understand myself.

Another component to this toxic potion was alcohol. It's so crazy, because when I entered the relationship, I didn't drink at all. (I had had enough jungle juice and frat parties during my freshman year at Seton Hall University.) But as my relationship began to fall to pieces due to an endless, impossible cycle, I turned to the bottle. Tequila was my best friend. Patron to be specific. Do you remember in chapter two when I spoke about childhood memories of alcohol always being present, well not only was I a bartender by profession, but I was managing my pain and unhappiness at home. I drank at home, or bars, or clubs, or with friends, or at work! It got worse. There were a few very embarrassing black-out moments, which my ex wasn't too pleased about. We'd get into arguments about that, and he tried to tell me several times that I had a problem. Well, you can only imagine how that went. I cussed him out of course and asked how he could ever accuse me of being alcoholic! Like who bleep bleep are you talking to?! All he would say is that I couldn't control myself and was not aware of my cutoff point. He would say, " Why do you have to drink so much? Why don't you stop once you get to that point of feeling nice". My answer was, " I only had one too many, I know what I'm doing. We do this in my family. My whole family can drink. The women can drink men under the table". Just looking at this and typing this is unbelievable to me. I would boast about my ability to drink. Like, why was I proud of that? It was indeed true, and I'm not ashamed of my family at all, but why was I so proud to have been attacked by the generational curse? It got so bad that I was literally wearing my curse as a badge of honor.

All of that drinking and the lifestyle that came with drinking killed my confidence. I gained 50 lbs and I was still pretty, thank the Lord, but I did not believe how much I expanded, and not in the way God wanted me to. Guess what I did to deal with my unhappiness. You guessed it. I drank! I drank more and more and had a ton of sex. A lot of sex. I needed to feel good. Plus, if I didn't have anything else, I had confidence in the bedroom. I figured, yeah the relationship is sour, yeah we argue daily about nothing, but I know exactly what to do to smooth all this over. It was the only way I felt connected to him. It was the only thing that made me feel good. It was the only way I knew to deal with the pain. So, I would have sex, and the instant, and I mean the instant it was over, I felt all the weight and darkness again. I would look at him and see that our connection only lasted during the time we were under the sheets. Eventually the sex couldn't sustain the toxicity of the relationship, and he asked me for space ya'll! I couldn't take it! All the feelings of feeling unappreciated came flooding my brain. I never said it to him but I definitely thought, "After

ALLLLLLLLLLLL the things I've done for HIM, he gonna ask me for SPACE?" I chuckle as I type this because, sis, yes!! You were toxic! I, however, did not find anything remotely humorous about the situation at the time. I was freaking out. I was also QUEEN PETTY. Space? You want space, what is space? A break? My simple self let him know, there were no "breaks" to be taken. I was not about to play on and off with anyone's son. So I gave him an ultimatum, another unhealthy test. Either stay and work this out or be done with me forever. I told him to think about if he really wanted to throw away everything we'd built like I hadn't already demolished it with my pride and insecurities. The guilt trip worked, he stayed. I want y'all to know that after some much-needed time with God and healing, I apologized and took accountability for my actions, because I really had no clue about the monster he was dealing with at the time.

So he stayed, and I stayed. I was elated because I thought, "Man, he really does love me! We can work this out and we will be fine." I neglected all the damage that had already been done. I had caused him so much emotional trauma, and trapped him in a relationship that he no longer desired to be part of, at the expense of him. As a result, resentment became the tone of our relationship. He started to become very short and disconnected from me. I definitely noticed and I began overcompensating to try and reel him back in. When my attempts failed, I became livid, more drunk, and more toxic. I noticed that he would sabotage our relationship. He would do things that he knew would be sure to push the red buttons on my heart so that I had a reason to want to leave. He was really trying to get out but I was not having it! I also began sabotaging the relationship as if I didn't do enough damage. However, my reasons for sabotage differed. My pride would not have anyone having a one up on me. So when my girlfriends sent me pictures of him at a club, hugged up with a girl, I'd go out of state, get drunk at a house party and get loose with a childhood friend. I'd never tell him. But I had the satisfaction of knowing, I'd outdone him! The problem with this is that I would return from my mischief with the burden of guilt. There were two versions of me when I looked at him. One that felt sorry for him being in this relationship and the other side that was angry at him, blaming him for my acts of pettiness, while also having the satisfaction that she'd not been outdone. SICK! I thank God for deliverance. Jesus!!!!

And so this toxicity became more potent. I continued to drink as much as my liver could handle and my partner became more and more distant from me. To top it all off, we stopped having sex! This, I could NOT handle. It became very clear to me that the space he desired was coming either way. I blamed him for staying with me even though I had manipulated him to do so. To feed my own pride, I decided to move across the country to Los Angeles, without consulting him, and told him that the space was coming, and for real this time. So I ran. I ran from the heartache, the pain, the insecurity, the accountability, and the alcohol. I stopped drinking when I moved to LA.

This chapter addresses generational curses because we have to know that they exist whether we understand they exist or not. I was aware of alcoholism. Almost all of the women in my family have dealt with this before. In fact, my great grandmother who lived with my mother, grandmother, and all of my aunts and uncles, was what you called a functioning alcoholic, rest her soul. This was a curse I had from both sides. While I didn't know much about my father, I did know that there was always a brown paper bag with a bottle present when he would come to pick me up and take me to my sister's house. I need yall to understand that these are not judgments but observations. It's important to go back to your foundation to see what it is that you may have picked up through observation. It is the very way we learn. I knew about alcoholism, but I was unaware of the pride, inability to listen, and feelings of unworthiness. Just because I wasn't aware of them, didn't mean they didn't have a major influence over my life. They snuck in and unfolded in a season where I was unprepared. I thank God for the time He's allowed us to have together and for His revelations. Because I'm aware of them, I gave them all to Him and He has given me authority over those demons, demons I wouldn't have noticed if I never made those wrong turns and endured some pain.

CHAPTER 4

It's Just The Way I Am
(False Identity)

And so now I live in LA. You may wonder how I ended up there, of all places. So if we rewind a bit, you'll find that I was a music major at Essex County College in Newark, New Jersey and just short of two classes from graduation. Some people may not deem a community college Associate's degree as a big deal, but for the overachieving high school president, a 4.0 all her life student that had only completed her freshman year at a borderline ivy league school, who watched her friends surpass her while she worked two jobs in the food industry, this was huge! It was a sign of completion. It was proof that for once I could actually finish something that I started. One day in the music wing, where I spent most of my time at ECC, I saw a poster for a school called AMDA, The American Musical & Dramatic Academy. This one poster stood out from the collage of posters on the wall. It had a halo or something. When I saw it, I felt my dream come back to life. I felt that there was an opportunity for a fresh start, a chance to get back on track. I've been singing since I was three. I was in a music group, recording my own lyrics and performing at 15, and had been taking courses in drama and film production while majoring in Music at ECC. My boyfriend at the time was a fellow musician and we created music together as well. I had even landed my first off broadway role in a production called Diva Dinners. So when I saw this poster, it made sense. I thought that this would be the answer to all my problems.

After some research, I noticed how intense the curriculum was. I was very intrigued. I had enough wisdom, even from my high school days, to know that I would never reach my potential unless I pursued the arts because school was just too easy. Where most kids struggled, I excelled. I was never nervous about tests. My best friend since age 12 hated school! I loved it! I looked forward to learning. I've always had an uncanny hunger for knowledge. I've gotten called a nerd so many times and I've always loved the title. I could give minimum effort and excel beyond my peers. My teachers would put me on a pedestal and praise me. This part I didn't like. I felt guilty for their praises and I knew my classmates were annoyed. I felt guilty because I didn't have to work hard or study! In fact, I hated studying. I was just graced with the gift of comprehension and memory. If you taught me something, and I understood it, I had it. Period. My mother made sure to let me know that I wasn't "smart" just because something came easy and that I should earn my accolades." So yes, I knew that the arts were the only outlet that would require me to forfeit my laziness. In the arts, if you don't work, you don't succeed. If you don't practice, you stay mediocre. If you don't learn discipline, then you fail. AMDA's curriculum was so demanding that I was sure of my success and was excited to finally be challenged. Don't get me wrong, I was certainly being challenged as a music major. I was learning music theory, sight-reading/singing, piano, jazz ensemble, and singing in the choir. It was WORK! I was also being challenged in my relationship in a way that made me too uncomfortable and instead of trying to actually work through the issues, I was, you know, becoming a raging alcoholic.

    I decided to audition for the school. This was a component I was unused to. I had to allow someone the opportunity to tell me no. I never let anyone or anything stop me. It was just the way I was. I wouldn't let my boyfriend tell me no in our relationship. I wouldn't let my boss tell me no when I wanted to move up the restaurant chain from hostess to bartender. I literally created my own training schedule until I could become a bartender. But here I was about to audition. I was confident in my acting abilities. I caught the acting bug bad! In fact, there was only one drama course, which I took four times and had the school create different levels on my transcript. You could say that I like to have my way. I set up the audition, told my boyfriend about it the day before and asked him to accompany me. Stop judging me!! It was part of my process. I didn't tell him because I didn't want to give him a chance to change my mind. Instead, I decided to make a decision and asked him whether or not he would be on board. I was still queen petty of unfair ultimatums. It was just the way I was.

    I was less than prepared for the audition. It was in New York. I overslept, it was raining and there was no parking. I threw on an outfit because I didn't know how to dress for an audition. I wore black jeans, a sheer black and white striped shirt and hooped earrings. The auditioner let me know that my shirt was too busy and my earrings were too distracting, a big no-no. I also miscredited one of my audition pieces, which I was corrected on. It's so funny to think about because the piece I led with was not one I worked on in class. It was one that a fellow classmate was assigned, but I was so arrogant that I failed to properly research it. The piece I had actually been assigned though, went off without a hitch. I had a special connection with *Camae* from *The Mountaintop* by Katori Hall.

    I waited for two weeks to hear back from the school. I heard nothing. Two weeks turned into a month and one month turned into two. It was coming up at the end of the year and I began to think that I just didn't have what it took. I felt like I would have to continue on with my destructive sad life, but something in me (which now I recognize as the Holy Spirit) was like, they still haven't said NO. So I called the admissions office and asked if they had any word of a decision for me. I was also a big procrastinator, so I had some paperwork lagging behind that may not have reached the admissions office. The woman on the phone let me know that they had indeed received all of my paperwork and my file showed that it was pending in the system. She also let me know that I would be getting a decision the following day. I was so anxious yall! The very next day I received a congratulatory email welcoming me to the school. I was elated! I was like, "FINALLY!" . All of the pieces were finally coming together. My high quickly plummeted once I realized what saying YES meant. I was leaving school two months from graduation. I was going to have to leave my entire family on the East coast. I was going to have to get rid of everything in my apartment and ship my baby Macy across the way. I was going to have to say goodbye to all of my friends who became my family during my 5 years in Jersey. I was going to have to finally say goodbye to my boyfriend of four years, after everything we gave to each other. I was about to change my life forever with one single "YES".

As if the mental and emotional stress of switching gears wasn't enough, there was a financial component that came with the transition. One that had dramatically halted my plans in the past at my first college. I became fearful that my dream would be crushed before I even got a chance to try. I had to decide that nothing would get in my way, not money, not relationships, and definitely not me! It was just the way I was! I was not going to take no for an answer. At this time I was also in my second off-broadway production. I was in an ensemble in a production of Dreamgirls, where I felt I should have been Effie White! I felt that life was imitating art. It was February and the semester began in June. That gave me four months to come up with the $22,000 plus that I needed to move. I walked into work one day after calculating everything on my kitchen counter and sat in my boss's office. I let him know that I had indeed been accepted to the school and that I needed to dramatically increase my funds in a short span of time. He was excited for me and agreed to have me on the schedule for as many hours as humanly possible. I appreciate you JK!

As my four months came to a close, my relationship became more and more strenuous. There were more arguments about nothing, more resentment and more drinking. I had a going-away party at a local pub in Jersey where my work family came to wish me farewell. I was very intoxicated and very emotional. After I said my goodbyes, I went home with my boyfriend. I attempted to seduce him. As we began having sex I became overwhelmed. Every moment we had together flashed through my mind like a whirlwind and I began to sob uncontrollably. I couldn't stop apologizing. I was very aware that I had caused both of us so much turmoil and here I was about to break our hearts again as my voyage into lands unknown was just one week away. This is still one of my saddest memories to date. We held each other and cried as we mourned the end of us.

My super supportive family and friends in Chester threw me another trunk party. I had one when I went away the first time. I was so overwhelmed by all of the support. I can say that I truly have been blessed to always have a strong support system. If I ever felt like I couldn't do something, they were always there to let me know that I was indeed fearfully and wonderfully made. I think much of my confidence came from their support. The time had come. It was time to board my flight to California. It was time to travel to uncharted territory. I would pick up my entire life to move to a school I never visited and relocate to a place I never had any interest in moving prior to seeing a poster.

This was just the way I was.

I was so proud of myself for daring to do the wild thing. I was proving to myself and everyone, my friends, family, coworkers, and ex that I had what it took. I was still going to make it, even if it meant leaving a "safe" point in my life. Many people admired what I was doing, and so did I. I wasn't fearful at all. This was a trait that I admired about myself. While I was far from God at this point, I never let go of His promise that I was fearfully and wonderfully made. I also held onto the promise that He did not give me a spirit of fear, but of power, love and a sound mind. That, my Mom Mom made sure it was instilled in me. These promises turned me into a fighter. I was raised by strong, black queens who knew how to stand on their own two feet and not accept defeat. I would follow suit. So, when my departing flight was canceled twice, hotel and car rental reservations canceled, and Macy packed with ALL of my belongings went missing, I fought! I was thinking," look how busy the devil is, trying to stop me before I even start! I eventually got settled into my new dorm and my car showed up two weeks into class. I was so excited for a fresh start. I'd had my boss in New Jersey talk to the proprietor in the same company a few miles from campus to help me secure a job. Things were finally looking good. It was hot in California and all 50 lbs that I gained felt the heat. I decided to hire a personal trainer to help me get my revenge body. Ladies, you know what that is. It's the super sexy version of yourself that you become so you can post on IG and show your ex how much he messed up. I was determined to thrive in all areas. I would make a name for myself at AMDA and eventually LA and I would be snatched! My ex was going to see, they would all see! It was just the way I was!

There were so many problems with this" Imma show you" complex. My reasons for pursuing success were all wrong. Even when I falsely convinced myself that I was over my ex, and that I was doing this to be a role model for my siblings and family, and even that I was doing this for me, the motive was still wrong. I didn't even realize my modes of motivation were improper until about two weeks ago and it's 2020. I was so worried about proving what I *could* do, that I never asked God what *He wanted* me to do. If I were to ask Him, I'm positive He would have given me this revelation earlier. But because I failed to deal with the pain from the earlier chapters of my life, I just ran to different modes of pain management. I threw myself into school and exercised to prove, prove, prove and when I didn't receive recognition from who I wanted it from the most, I still felt unachieved. I wanted to be seen so badly! I was literally in multiple acting classes daily with an audience, receiving great feedback from people I watched on TV as a kid and it still wasn't enough. My first acting teacher literally had us repeat the mantra," I am whole, I am enough, I am a great actor." It still wasn't enough! My friends and family continuously applauded my efforts for taking a chance and following my dreams, but it wasn't enough! And here's why. The only "job well done" that matters comes from God. Take a moment to let that sink in. The only opinion of you that matters is God's.

CHAPTER 5

Only God Can Judge Me (Yet I Judge Myself)

There were so many differences between my new life in LA and my life in New Jersey. The weather, for one, was exquisite! I loved that it was sunny 99.9% of the time. I loved the fact that I could actually travel a mile away to Runyon Canyon and hike mountains overlooking the entire city. I was in a different time zone, I was single, abstinent and free from the grips of alcoholism. I found myself on the up and up. I was attending classes where I had to be vulnerable and judged. It was so surreal. In Jersey, I rarely allowed anyone an opportunity to have any say over anything I did, but here I was anxiously awaiting critique and constructive criticism. Could this be growth? All of my professors were working professionals in the industry. I understood that the critique they gave me could be trusted and that I was their student. What teacher doesn't want their student to succeed? It felt different from high school where I found myself being persecuted by some students and teachers alike for my gifts. It was different from growing up in my home where my younger brother waited on me to slip up as we competed for my mother's attention. Here, at performing arts school, mess-ups were encouraged and then corrected. All of my teachers encouraged us to make BIG choices. I got that note so many times. "You can be bigger, you can be bolder, don't play it safe". They really wanted to break us out of our shells. My teachers were fellow artists. They understood the hardships that come with the industry struggles like rejection and not feeling good enough. Each of my 30+ teachers drilled into us that we were indeed perfect and whole, even if we didn't get a role. They created a safe environment where we practiced trial and error. They wanted us to break free from self-judgment!

This aspect of the arts was so difficult for me. While I may have relocated, the strain of not feeling "good enough" still sat with me, even though my teachers and classmates continuously praised my talents. Sometimes I felt like they were just saying nice things to encourage me. I could not seem to grasp that I was actually talented or actually growing as an artist. Even though I diligently studied my scripts and memorized them. I added tactics and actions and made each character come to life in my own way, even when I did everything we were instructed to do, I could not believe that I was good enough. I was still getting straight A's, this time for performance, and it still wasn't good enough. It's so strange to think about how confident I looked to everyone on the outside, well at least to my peers. My teachers saw right through my facade and continued challenging me to go deeper and make bigger choices. They assured me that it was ok to make a wrong choice, but the truth is, I was still terrified of suffering from wrong choices. I began combing over my life and remembering all of my bad choices and how they negatively affected me and those connected to me. I thought about how I'd mistreated my ex. I thought about how AMDA was my third college and was now becoming a "professional student". I thought about how far away I was from my family and my baby brother. I thought about how I lashed out at his father and gave him a piece of my mind for the pain he caused my family in my teenage years. I thought about how I went to school trying to follow a boy who ended up attending a different school altogether. I thought about how I gave my first boyfriend my virginity though I vowed to be pure and wait for my husband. I didn't want to make any more bold choices. I didn't believe it was safe. I judged myself for all the "bad" choices made, and here were my teachers telling me to be as big and bold as I could be.

I was holding onto my good girl complex I had adopted since childhood, so I remained playing it safe. Playing it safe felt good, but not really. Every time I left a scene I'd say, "I wish I would've made a bigger choice. I wonder what would have happened if I put in a little more work, or tried this". I was judging myself for not making bigger choices while telling myself not to color outside of the lines, quite the conundrum. I didn't realize that my inability to choose anything was keeping me stagnant and causing me to feel scattered. I found it difficult to connect with the characters. I even began to judge them! (Which is a huge faux pa in the acting world) If you judge the character, rather than trying to understand the life that has created the character's point of view, a connection is unattainable. In the same way, I couldn't connect with myself. I was ashamed of my past and refused to look my guilt in the face. I ran child! I ran 3,000 miles away from my pain and shame, but they still went to bed with me every night. Condemnation was having its way with me. I fought to push those feelings down deeper and deeper and my work continued to suffer. I still received good marks in class, but could not seem to get cast in any of the school's productions. So there I was, dealing with rejection on top of my harsh criticism! My own criticism made me begin to judge the work of my peers. We were supposed to create a safe space for one another to flourish, but I was busy being annoyed by the laziness, or unpreparedness, or poor choices. I secretly envied the students who were willing to make a fool out of themselves and my teachers applauded it. This made no sense to me and I became frustrated.

I avoided working with certain people and deemed them "attention whores". This was because instead of trying to understand them, or their reasons for being what I perceived as unnecessary, I harshly judged them. They felt my judgment I'm sure. There were more than a few people who felt uncomfortable performing in front of me. I used to think it was because they respected my work ethic and couth, but it was really because they were afraid to make a mistake in front of my judging eyes. I couldn't understand why in rehearsals, students who normally were outgoing and carefree, were quiet and calculated when it came to me. This also frustrated me! I'm like you know what, I'm gonna find more people who will work hard, study and prepare. They would be my scene partners because I could not settle for anything less than excellent. I went looking for my fellow fearless perfectionists (an oxymoron). I was doing the same thing I was doing in Jersey.

You've heard of the saying, "Birds of a feather flock together". It's so true. I wanted to be comfortable in my stagnancy, so I would seek out groups of people who wouldn't challenge me to go bigger. I looked for people who would work very hard, cross all the I's and dot all the T's , but wouldn't dare to do more than that for the fear of looking wrong. It's the same thing that alcoholics do. They surround themselves with other alcoholics so their problem seems like normality. It becomes everyone else on the outside who has a problem. You begin to take pride in your problem so much that others start to wonder if they're missing out or doing something wrong because you display this false sense of hyper-confidence. You dress up the issues at hand and make them look really attractive to the point you begin to believe that your way is the right way and everyone else better get with the program. And anyone who threatens to rise up against your mighty facade will get the business. You viciously protect your comfort zone, and anyone who doesn't agree will be blocked or removed. You begin to expect people to know who you are and how you operate, so they better not try it!

CHAPTER 6

Don't Try Me (Living with Offense)

As you're reading this, you're probably beginning to realize that if pain is not properly dealt with, it shapes you in an undesirable way, and that is exactly what began to occur in my life. I became extremely defensive of my self-constructed wall that protected my insecurities. I was truly a savage. I walked around with this false sense of confidence that made people feel inferior. I got a kick out of it too. My acting skills were so advanced that my facade became believable. I was prepared to battle anyone who would dare to call me out. Have you ever met a person who walked around with a, "I wish you would" complex? That was me. Most times I would only have to look at someone in a certain way because the intensity of my subdued pain could be felt in my glare. That didn't stop some people from provoking me. I hated to be provoked. I was very aware of my sharp tongue and the damage that it could do from my previous relationship. I didn't want to be reminded of the hurt that I caused him, but I also would not shy away from any challenge brought before me. In fact, I used people's boldness toward me as an opportunity to make an example out of them. This was to let anyone else know, that if you dared to cross the line with me, you would indeed walk away limping. I was also very prideful so there was no room for apologies. "I'm sorry that you thought it was okay to get above yourself and challenge me", that was really how I thought.

Some people were entertained by my sass and sarcasm that would end a rebuttal before it even got a chance to take flight. I shut down and dismissed people so quickly and effectively, it became a sport, a sport that I enjoyed. It made me feel powerful. I felt that people began to accept the way I was, but it was only because I didn't leave much room for any other options. You remember, "Queen Petty" of unfair ultimatums. I really meant it when I said, "get on board, get out of the way, or get moved!." Naturally, I wasn't afraid of any kind of challenge, definitely not people. I was still afraid of pain though. While my personal life became more painful, I became more vicious. In my second semester, we were about to demo Tarantella for Voice Production & Speech class when I got a terrifying call from my mother. She told me that my 26-year cousin had passed away from an accidental overdose. I was in disbelief at this news, not him! What about his two young children? How could he be gone at 26? I was 23, just three years younger and dealing with the guilt of leaving my family in the first place. Here I was on the other side of the country running from pain and chasing a dream while my cousin lay lifeless, locked in a room alone. Instead of allowing myself to have a human experience, I immediately went into robot mode while I forcefully repeated, "Do you remember an inn Miranda, do you remember an inn?" over and over in my mind. I sat stoically in my chair as I thought about what news I'd received. Some even asked if I was ok, and I dryly responded," I'm good, thanks". I was not good. My heart was breaking yet again as I sat in that chair, but the fear of experiencing grief's pain was something I would not let overcome me. The teacher finally called my name. I stood on the mark placed on the floor while I blankly stared at the wall and took a deep breath. I hardly remember the performance. I just remember staring at the wall with my lips moving. I was numb and didn't want to feel anything.

    Later in my dorm, I called my mom to learn what actually happened. My cousin was on house arrest at the time and I believe he was depressed. I couldn't imagine my cousin who was always dancing, burning on us and making us laugh to the point of tears, sitting in a room lifeless. I attempted to recall our final encounters. He told me that he loved me and was proud of me. I smiled as I looked into his beautiful green eyes surrounded by red clouds. I saw something that wasn't there when we were kids. I knew he smoked weed. I also had begun smoking weed by now but never imagined that he had been taking pills or sipping lean. Unknowingly taking pills with conflicting chemistries took his life. My family was deeply saddened by this. It's never supposed to be one of the kids. My cousins and I were all raised like siblings. This new dynamic I could not accept; I wouldn't accept it because accepting that meant experiencing the pain that came with it.

It's so important to deal with pain in a healthy way. If you're reading this and you or someone you know is abusing promethazine or pills of any kind, please seek help. It's so unfortunate to make a permanent decision to solve a temporary problem. Mental health and depression are real issues that should not be taken lightly. It's dangerous to use artificial vices to lighten the burden of pain. That is why it's important first to talk to God. Talk to Him because He heals all pain. If you're not confident in Him yet, seek counseling or talk to a loved one with good judgment. I wonder how talking to someone would have changed my cousin's outcome. Life does get hard at times. Some storms may seem like they'll never end but you have to know that everything happens in seasons. You also have to be aware that your actions do indeed have consequences, some of which are irreversible. I still pray for healing over his mother, siblings and entire family. May I ask that you also lift my family in prayer?

When I traveled home for the funeral, I was relieved to be back in the loving arms of my family, but sad about the occasion. I sang at his funeral. I cried a lot. I let out a lot of pain that I had been holding onto since my move to LA. I finally felt like it was safe to just breathe. I felt like I didn't have to apologize for being "weak". I was allowed to be myself in that moment with no borders, no facades, only pain, and it didn't kill me.

CHAPTER 7

You Owe Me An Apology (Bitterness)

As the end of the second semester came to a close, I became anxious. Anxious because I would be heading back to the east coast post the semester break. I would be living in New York, a place I frequently partied while living in Jersey, but I could never actually see myself living there. While I loved the hustle and bustle of the east coast, New York was a different, overpopulated, and expensive beast. It is truly the city that never sleeps. AMDA has two campuses, one in Los Angeles and one in New York. If you're registered for a BFA program, there is an opportunity to experience what they call "NYE- New York Experience" which entails an even more vigorous curriculum for your third semester. With the recent passing of my cousin, I jumped at the opportunity to be so close to home. Plus, I was ready to dive into what I knew would be a life-changing semester. I must admit that I was excited to show off the 30 pounds that I shaved off to my New Jersey crew, and my ex. He was going to be sorry for letting me leave. I was sure of it.

During the break, I started to let people know that I would be close and couldn't wait to reconnect. However, after my first day of the New York orientation, it became very clear that the majority of my time would be spent challenging myself in ways that I had never experienced! I was literally overwhelmed by all of the information, books, and requirements. Our new schedule left us very little time to eat, sleep, or hide from pain. It took too much energy to hide from real life. All of my acting skills had to be reserved for the stage. While I was closer to my family, I rarely had time for phone calls, let alone home visits. My days started at 6 a.m. and ended at 11 p.m. or later every night, and yet, I managed to find time to check in with my ex.

Even with my new demanding schedule, I was very anxious about seeing him. I wanted him to experience the new and improved me and to see how he was *really* doing. His social media looked like he was partying and having a wonderful time, but I knew him and knew that he was actually hurting and dealing with our breakup in an unhealthy way. I figured, if I could sit down and talk with him, we could both get some closure and talk about underlying issues now that we'd had some time apart. Tracking him down however, was nearly impossible. I began to feel like he was avoiding me. He no longer worked at the job we previously worked together, and his group of friends had changed. My friends, however, had a close eye on him and made sure to update me about his new dating habits. They'd tell me that he was associating with some very interesting ladies. They couldn't understand why he was taking interest in them, but I did. It was rebound season. Similarly, I'd had my own rebound season when I voyaged to LA.

A detour:

Initially, I was tackling school with a sense of hyper-focus to compensate for the guilt, shame and pain. While I was able to replace alcohol with exercise, my sexual appetite did not subside. The problem with using sex as a security blanket is that the craving strengthens with each encounter. Sex is a very powerful, physical, emotional and spiritual experience, making it difficult to forget. My flesh became antsy, and so I turned to Tinder. This was a very new experience for me. The only men I'd been with were my ex and my high school boyfriend. Before that, I wanted to be celibate and pure for marriage. From a young age, the idea of giving myself to multiple people was very disturbing. I was sometimes curious about what it would be like to be with other men while I was with my ex, but not curious enough to become "loose". My friends would always ask me how I knew what I liked if I didn't have others to compare to. I didn't want a comparison. I knew what felt good to me and I liked to experiment within the confines of my relationship. I couldn't wrap my mind around increasing my body count, especially into the teens like many of my peers. But there I was, turning to Tinder. It's amazing how some pain and unpleasant experiences can influence your values.

After swiping left or right for a couple of weeks, I matched with someone who met my criteria, you know, tall, chocolate, round lips and pretty teeth. In fact, that was my nickname for him, "Pretty Teeth". We went on a beautiful beach date where we talked and enjoyed each other's company. We did drink a little bit and we definitely smoked. California's weed is very different from the weed on the East Coast. I had tried smoking three or four times in New Jersey, but it never really became a habit. It was illegal for one, and I wasn't knowledgeable enough to smoke alone. But in Cali, it was easily accessible and more common than cigarettes. Weed has its own culture, one of community and calmness (which was great because I felt alone and lacked peace). And so we smoked and kissed under the stars on the beach. Pretty Teeth was an amazing kisser and our chemistry was electric. I was very surprised that I could even feel this with another person. I thought that I was so heartbroken, that I wouldn't be able to connect with another man, especially in such a short period of time. But we were indeed connected, and my flesh started to feel things it hadn't felt in a long time. The feeling was too strong, strong enough for me to ask him if I could come in when we returned to his home after the beach. He was a little hesitant because his visually impaired grandmother also resided there. I didn't care about who was in there! I was ready to scratch that itch, besides she couldn't put a name to a face. She didn't know me. Our physical chemistry continued to magnify as we became more intimate and less clothed. I felt like a virgin, touched for the very first time, and in a way I was. This was my first time experiencing sex while high and I wondered why I hadn't experienced before. Stella had gotten her groove back y'all! I felt, "This is perfect!". I had no desire to be in a relationship and no time either. School was going well, I was working out and now I had a Cali bae who was fine and sexually compatible.

If this sounds too good to be true, it's because it was. My habits of selfishly using sex still existed. I didn't talk to Pretty Teeth much and when I did it was only concerning the next time we would get together and knock boots. I was so caught up in my desires, that I was neglecting him and his feelings. I didn't even notice that he was beginning to fall for me, until one day. It was a weekend day, maybe Saturday or Sunday, and I'd been lustful all week. I had about an hour and a half until I had to clock in, and tardiness was not an option. I tried to ignore my urge, but it was too strong. I made some calculations and discovered that if I left at that moment, I'd have just enough time to get some and get to work. I sent Pretty Teeth a 911 and let him know that I was on my way. He greeted me with kisses when I arrived and attempted to engage in conversation, a normality with us, but I couldn't afford time for small talk. The more he spoke, the more I stopped his lips with mine. " I'm pressed for time sir". I think I actually asked him if we could just get to it. After I got my fix, I jumped up to redress. When I looked over at him, he looked sad and disturbed. I frowned my brows out of confusion and then he said something to me that I would never forget. " You mind as well leave the money on the dresser since that's what you came here for". I was bamboozled. What? I assured him that it wasn't like that but I really had to get to work, but he was uninterested in what I had to say.

On my drive to work, I became annoyed and confused. I started to play the blame game. "How could he think we were serious? We met on Tinder! We slept together on the first date!". Confusion overwhelmed me. I thought this is what guys wanted, to have sex with a beautiful girl, no commitments, and no strings attached! Yet, here he was trying to make me feel guilty? I added someone to my body count and we weren't even going to continue sleeping together. The more I thought about it, the worse I felt. It's never fun hurting anyone or making someone feel less than. I did just that by using someone to satisfy my own desires. I felt terrible about how I treated him. He began ignoring me which made me even angrier. I still had a craving, but I decided it wasn't worth it. I was going to be abstinent. I started to remember my earlier attitudes towards sex and purity, and why they were in place. Sex is too powerful to be used immaturely, escpecially as a tool of manipulation. I owed him an apology.

End of detor:

After some detective work, I found out where my ex was working and decided I would visit him. Whenever he would respond to me, he'd claim to be busy or at work, and if he was still a work-a-holic like I remembered, I'd be sure to find him. I was correct. One night I hopped on a bus, over the bridge to Jersey. My first stop would be my old job to visit my work family and to inquire about picking up some weekend shifts. I was literally a starving artist in New York and needed the funds. My girls met me at the job and brought me current on what had transpired since I left. After dinner and a margarita or two, I headed to his workplace. It was about 11 p.m. when I walked through the doors of his job, duffle bag in hand. Yes, I had a duffle bag. I was going to be in Jersey for the weekend, unsure of where I would be staying, but I had a backup in case my plan backfired. They were definitely closing, which I could tell from the hostess' expression when I asked to be seated with him. I anxiously waited for him to walk up and see me. I imagined what our reunion would be like after 6 months, the longest amount of time we'd been apart from each other in four years. I felt him approach me from behind. I smiled to turn around and to my unpleasant surprise, it was not my ex, at all. It was a pretty girl smiling back at me. Confusion! I continued to smile as I ordered another margarita and asked for the dessert menu. Who was this girl and why was she serving me when I asked for him? It didn't take long to make the connection, but my thought process was interrupted when my ex walked up, looking like he'd seen a ghost. This was not how I envisioned our reunion. He stood still for a few moments as the realization set in. She's baaaack. He asked me, "Why I didn't let him know that I was coming?" I let him know I wasn't going to give him an opportunity to run from me, "classic, crazy Asia". (I'm sure this is what he was thinking, and I get it, but I cancel that word curse over my life in Jesus name!) He commented on my weight loss, and I was pleased he noticed because I struggled with my weight in our relationship. In the midst of our awkward reacquaintance, my waitress returned with a menu, interrupting our reunion and serving him a "look". "She's cute", I said as I sipped my margarita. He said that she was "the homie". Y'all know I didn't buy it, but I had no concern for her or who she was. I was back here and so was he, and that's all that mattered. I asked him what he was doing after work. I figured we could catch up. He let me know that it would be about an hour before he was done closing up. I should've taken that as a hint, but wasn't going to allow him to get away. You were not going to avoid me sir! I told him I'd take time with my dessert and wait for him to finish. I think he recognized that this was a battle I would not lose, so he obliged.

After he finished his closing duties, he approached my table to let me know. I paid the bill and thanked his "homie" for her service and wished her a good night. I don't really remember the ride to his apartment, but I imagine it was awkward and filled with small talk. I didn't want to talk much, a new skill I learned in acting school. I would be quiet and observant. Everything that I wanted to know would reveal itself.

Walking into his apartment resurrected memories of the last time. The last time I was here, we lay in bed crying and holding one another. The time before that we had a huge argument about one of his female classmates who kept showing up in his snapchats and in my friend requests on Instagram. I threw his keys at him and stormed out. I remembered arguments over food that he didn't want to share when I shared everything. I remembered an argument that came from being restricted to a certain side of the bed. I looked at my furniture from my apartment that was now in his room and remembered how upset I was when he complained of helping me move it out of my place. All I could remember were bad memories and it made me sad, very sad. I was still very quiet, and he noticed. I wanted to be there so bad, and now that I was, I was extremely uncomfortable. He went to shower and my discomfort grew with more observation. I noticed a pair of lashes with a healthy strip of glue next to the TV. I noticed a questionable stain on the sheets. I looked in the dresser drawer and found condoms. It started to become very clear why he was so busy all of the time. I wanted to jump down his throat and raise hell as I was accustomed to before, but I decided against it. If I wanted honest answers from him, I would have to adjust my approach.

When he returned from the shower, I was practically hanging off the corner of the bed. When he inquired about my position, I let him know that I noticed a mysterious stain in the sheets and suggested he should wash them. I studied him waiting for a response, but never got one. Enough said. I stood up to head to the shower. As I showered I began to ask myself why I was there and what my plan was. I was uncomfortable and it was too late to go anywhere else. I'd gotten exactly what I wanted, and I didn't want it. Was I really going to sleep there? What did I expect to happen? I couldn't wait to go to work in the morning. I returned from the shower and asked for a T-shirt. I started to grab one from where I remembered they were but he jumped up to stop me, letting me know he would get it and making it clear about which side I stood on concerning the boundaries in his life. I'd already crossed one showing up at his job. I dropped my towel and began to apply lotion. This weight loss was going to be seen! As I lotioned my body I noticed that the lashes that lay on the table had disappeared. I saw him watching in my peripheral and sure as I saw him he commented on my appearance and ended up entangled in his bed. This encounter with him was very different from all of our previous ones. Things occured that never had before in our four years together which further confirmed my suspicions about him being with other women. I was uncomfortable and when it was over, I laid there sad. I felt like I didn't know him anymore. I was also upset at myself for sleeping with him, knowing what I knew. I was angry at him for allowing the encounter when he knew that he was seeing other people. I felt like he owed me an apology, even though I pursued him. The following morning, I got up to get dressed and I could see him watching me, still in disbelief at my transformation, but I was disgusted. I was disgusted with him and myself and I was ready to get out. I felt like he had used me like he used those other girls to take out his pain, like I used Pretty Teeth. Hurt people really do hurt people, but hurt people also seek out more hurt in the search for love.

CHAPTER 8

Do You Love Me (Searching for Love)

Despite the unpleasant encounter, I still continued to reach out to him. This was still someone I spent four years of my life with and still had an incredible amount of love for. I assumed that he also had a love for me, partly because this is what I was told. Living in LA afforded me time to reflect on our relationship from an outside perspective. I concluded that even though we may have caused each other some pain, love still had to be present in some capacity. I began blaming myself for the way he was dealing with his pain, after all, I played a significant role in causing it. I felt responsible for his ongoing transformation and felt I needed to maintain a relationship, or at least a friendship, where we could aid one another into this new phase of life. This, however was problematic.

Every attempt to connect was met with intense resistance. The truth was absent from our conversations and I couldn't understand why his responses to me were short or delayed. When I questioned him about seriously dating anyone, his "homie" from the job in particular, he repeatedly denied my accusations, but I knew what it felt like when he lied to me. Every time we planned to link up, even just to talk, something would "come up". He'd visit New York without mentioning anything to me and my feelings became hurt. I understood that we were no longer in a romantic relationship. After everything we'd been through, couldn't we at least salvage the friendship? The answer was no. Too much damage had been done and eventually his "homie" became his girlfriend, which he let me know later in a text message, explaining his distance tactics to me. I, of course, was infuriated. I couldn't understand why he would lie about something I already knew. We weren't together and I didn't expect us to rekindle any extinguished flames. Was he trying to protect me? Was he trying to protect her? What remained of my crushed feelings led me to accept that I no longer had any weight in his life. I wished him the best and deleted him from my social media accounts. I couldn't handle seeing him with someone else. How could he be in a real relationship so soon? I deemed him desperate and became jealous. The person I knew was dissipating day by day and I wanted nothing to do with him. I was going to have to thrive all alone and let him watch me rise to the top with the rest of the crowd. I was hurt, bitter, jealous and in denial of it all. The only thing that I was sure about was that we were over and for real this time.

I couldn't believe that I had become someone's "Ex" for the second time, that I had become insignificant to someone who at one point loved me so deeply. I never understood how people could exit a relationship and take their love back. It's no way it was that easy, it wasn't for me. If I love you, I love you forever. How could it be that I struggled to purge my mind and heart from memories of them and they could go along with their lives as if we never existed? I felt the way I did when I was 18, after calling it quits with my first boyfriend. I began to remember the feelings of disappointment and disbelief. I remember feeling like I would never get over him because I gave him all of me. I struggled to pinpoint where our relationship began shifting but to no end. I became addicted to closure, a closure that only comes from acceptance and forgiveness. I was in no position to forgive anyone. Instead, I wanted to blame him and victimize myself by justifying my hurt feelings. "How could he love me so childishly? How could he take my purity and run away? Did he forget who I was?". No, I forgot who I was and *whose* I was. My self-worth was measured by the way I let people love me, failing to realize that my true identity and value lay in who

I was in God. When you're hurt and heartbroken, it's hard to feel like you have a royal crown. You're tempted to find your worth in superficial things like looks, social acceptance, relationships, talents, and money. The truth is that all of those things will make you feel inadequate upon achieving them, because your motive to get them is to prove to your past lover how much they messed up. All the while, you're messing yourself up. I messed myself up!

After I graduated high school, I partied and got drunk the entire summer. I was so heartbroken over my first boyfriend I didn't know what to do. We had the same group of friends so it seemed like I couldn't get away from him even if I tried. I didn't want to be away from him though. Every time we saw each other, I hoped that he would remember me, and see the girl he fell in love with once upon a time. It never happened. We all went off to college, spreading out across the country which slipped me into a bout of depression. My best friend since the 7th grade had been shipped to Savannah, Georgia, and I couldn't feel love anywhere. I lost my passion for school and learning. I'd be on Facebook, stalking my friends or online shopping during class seminars, and it was reflected in my test scores. My transcripts consisted of grades I'd never experienced in my entire scholastic career, and I was on the brink of failing Psychology, my major at the time. I was unsure of who I was anymore but I knew I didn't like her. I couldn't focus, all I could do was re-live the heartbreak and attempt to remember the pleasantries of the good old days. I was convinced that my best days were behind me.

Love seemed to be a far-fetched fantasy for me. Even when I received attention from multiple guys, gullibility was not an option. My mind was convinced that boys were simply immature at my age, and they were all incapable of truly loving me. Flirting was still a hobby of mine but that's all that it was. Never again, would I open myself up to vulnerability to an undeserving child whose focus was to get into my pants. I would not be subjected to heartbreak for a second time. My lesson had been learned. Rejection and abandonment were things I was not willing to accept. Self-love was going to have to be sufficient, and for a while it was, until I returned home for semester breaks. Deep down, I had never accepted that my first boyfriend was no longer mine. I had given him my virginity and was soul-tied to him, making me incapable of breaking away from him. Subsequently, I continued to give myself to him. Each time was unpleasant, but I could not let him forget about me. I wanted to be memorable. I wanted him to think about me the same way I thought about him. I figured that even if he didn't admit it to me, I would be at the forefront of his thoughts. The love we shared could not have left without a trace, I wouldn't let it.

Holding onto the love that I had for my first boyfriend, and my refusal to become invisible to him caused problems in my following relationship. I'd known my college boyfriend a year before we began taking interest in one another. I had seen him around campus and had brief encounters with him at parties, but never experienced a substantial connection with him. Because I was so guarded, the possibility of entering another serious relationship seemed obsolete, but in the summer after our freshman year, something changed. We began to see each other in a new way, entering the "talking stage". You know what that is. It's the phase when one attempts to feel out a person. Our interest in each other grew quickly and bilaterally. We shared a common friend in whom we both confided. Our feelings for each other were uncanny. Every level of attraction and interest was mimicked by the other, but neither of us wanted to express our feelings at the risk of being too forward. Instead, we both confided in our common friend, who would come back to each of us, spilling what the other had told us. It wasn't until we went on a group outing that we were able to experience each other in a new way.

We, our common friend, and three of her friends went to Brooklyn for a Caribbean fest. We packed into my tiny car (Macy) as we drove to the event, forcing me to sit on his lap. I later discovered that this was all part of an elaborate scheme devised by our common friend. The festival was amazing! There was food, music, tons of people and elaborate costumes that resembled bathing suits. We were all having a good time when gunfire broke out amongst the crowd. People began to scream and scatter frantically and my crush grabbed my hand and took flight. It was at that moment that I knew I wanted to be with him. I was so impressed that he thought to protect me and guide me to safety. We were with three other guys and they only thought about themselves as they ran. After making our way back to the car, we headed back to one of the guy's apartments for our common friend to have a moment with him. As we sat on opposite sides of a couch, waiting for our friend, we discussed the crazy outing and fought our urges to kiss one another. I couldn't believe what I was feeling. As per usual, we later discussed our feelings for each other with our common friend, until we set up a date with just the two. I invited him to my apartment for a movie night. It was the first time we discussed our growing feelings, hearing the truth from each other rather than our common friend. It was also the night that we shared our first kiss. It was nothing short of magical and then frightening. I became afraid to the point of tears because here I was falling in love, and the last time I fell in love it ended in heartbreak that I was still dealing with. He noticed my discomfort and questioned me about it. I told him that I was afraid. He held me in his arms and reassured me that I had nothing to fear with him, so I decided to let myself fall deeper and harder than I ever had before, though heartbreak still haunted me.

    The first time we argued, fear encompassed me. I panicked and reached out to my high school ex to ask him if he could remember why we began falling off. It doesn't make much sense to me currently, but at the time I was doing damage control. I did not want to mess things up with my new boyfriend and I still longed for closure. It felt impossible to close the previous chapter without it. Our common friend shared with my boyfriend that I reached out to my ex which caused an insecurity in him. I wouldn't learn about this until years later during an argument between us concerning him. My boyfriend couldn't understand why I had to communicate with my ex. I pleaded with him as I tried to explain that I was friends with my ex before he was my boyfriend and still cared about him. It's true, I did care about him, and still do until this day, but it had more to do with my pride. My pride prohibited me from respecting my relationship. I didn't want him to forget me, not realizing that whether he did or didn't, wasn't of importance. It's not important today either. I had to learn that as long as God saw me, that's all that mattered. It was hard to get to this point of comfortability with accepting that I was only in someone's life for a season. It was my job to reflect on those seasons to get the lessons. If you truly love someone, you will let them go. If you truly love yourself, you won't subject yourself to your past, and allow yourself to transform into the version of you that God has called you to be.

    This is a concept that took me years to understand in my heart. Once I accepted that our relationship was over, I vowed to focus on me and me only. I would not waste any more love, time, finances, or energy to those who were unworthy of it. This time around, I was going to live for myself!

CHAPTER 9

It's All About Me (Selfishness)

Many people would agree that your twenties are your selfish years. It's a time for discovery, reflection, and rebuilding. While some of that may be true, being selfish did not mean canceling regard for everyone and everything around you. I already had a "don't get in my way" mindset, but when I decided to become selfish and only take care of myself, I became a different kind of monster. I literally did whatever made me happy, despite how anyone felt about it. If you weren't contributing to my happiness, I had no interest in you, at all. If you didn't want to participate in an activity that I wanted, then off we went, Me, Myself & I. I pushed myself to the max at school because I wanted to master my craft. I was going to soak up every ounce of knowledge and experience while making my tuition dollars count! I worked out and dieted like never before. My health became my primary focus as I continued to shed more weight. My money would be spent on me and me only. I demanded control over my thoughts. When they began to roam and recollect memories from the past I shifted the energy into productivity. I was determined to regain control of my life.

While many positive attributes came from being selfish, some negative ones did too. I became more aggressive and judgemental with my classmates. I'd pretty much decided who I was/wasn't willing to work with. If you were here to be lazy and stress me out, the door! Mediocracy was not an option for me or my work. I still had a healthy craving for sex, so pornography and masturbation became a nightly hobby. If it made me feel good, that's all I was concerned about. Consuming all of those images eventually led me to seek out a new sexual partner. It had been about a year since I decided to have my first` and only one-night stand. It was almost a year that I had been abstinent and felt I deserved to have a little fun. On my ex's birthday, in some sick twisted way, I convinced myself that I would have his "birthday sex" and it would be better than whoever he was experiencing. I did indeed have a great time. He made me feel good, for the moment, and I would never see him again. I'd added another body to my count, and I didn't even care. This should have been a warning sign that I was changing, and not for the better. I stopped reaching out to my family and friends. They would have to understand that I was simply too busy working on myself. They knew that I loved them. I felt so good about myself. "Look at me!", I thought. I'd finally let my hair down and gave myself some room to be a little messy. I began making bigger choices in life and at school. I purposely chose difficult material because I felt my classes lacked challenges after my rigorous New York Experience. I was finally living for myself! It was all about me and I loved it. My creativity came back and I found myself writing songs and scripts. I finally felt like the wheels were turning in a forward motion until I got news that stopped me in my tracks.

During my fourth semester, I received a call from my mom yet again, this time telling me that my Pop Pop had had a stroke and was in the hospital. Those words didn't fully register to me. A stroke? My Pop Pop was a healthy, hard-working man with all his witts. My Pop Pop was my father figure who fed my imagination with love and support from childhood. My Pop Pop provided me with Macy (my beloved 2003 Toyota Echo), car insurance, care packages and allowance. My Pop Pop was my get-out-of-jail-free card, should I ever hit rock bottom. How was he lying in a hospital bed? My mom video-called me from the hospital when she visited him. I couldn't believe what I was seeing. My hero, my strong working hands, Jessie James was lying still in a hospital bed with various tubes protruding from him. How could this have happened? What did this mean for my Mom Mom? What did it mean to me? My mom told me that they were monitoring him for a few days, but I couldn't handle a few days. I needed to feel happy, but that wasn't possible. I needed the next best thing, numbness.

    I had already been smoking socially, but it was at this point that I became a pothead. I would beat grief to the punch. I didn't want updates about what was happening, but that wouldn't stop them from coming. The guilt and grief of losing my cousin only a year prior revisited me, but it was no match for the weed. I smoked until I thought it was impossible to get any higher. I went from smoking three or four times per week to three or four times a day. This was going to have to be a new way of life. I didn't know how to deal with the shock and disbelief when I got the news that they were pulling the plug. I struggled to recall our final conversation. I was so busy with my selfish season, that I missed my chance to love on my Pop Pop a little more. I forfeited him telling me he loved me one more time. The pain that attempted to enter my being was too strong, so every time my high subsided I got high one more time.

    I flew home for another funeral, this time my Pop Pop's and I wondered what I did to deserve this. Why was my family under attack? I needed answers. Sitting at the funeral and watching my Mom Mom cry out to God in worship infuriated me. How could she praise the one who took him from us? Was she being strong, or was she in denial? All I could feel was hurt and sadness. I spoke at my Pop Pop's funeral, sharing anecdotes about my childhood and the unconditional love he shared with me. I looked down at him realizing he would never walk me down the aisle. It was at that moment that I looked up and saw my dad in the crowd. I became even more furious. Why was he here? What had he done for me? I was convinced that I was already in the process of burying my father. As I continued to share my stories of love and teaching concerning my Pop Pop, I couldn't help but wonder if my dad felt guilty that he hadn't taught me anything about love or fatherhood. I secretly wished that he felt convicted for his absence in my life, or maybe I hoped that he would finally realize that it was his turn to step up for me, that his daughter needed her father. It wasn't until then that I actually felt the void of having an absent father. I was too bitter to reach out and tell him what I desired to have from him. I figured he was the parent and should be the one to comfort and love his daughter. He wasn't exempt from my selfish attitude. The problem with this mindset is that he couldn't understand that I longed to have a relationship with him because I carried on like I was fine. I acted as if I didn't need anything from him. I'd been taught to stand on my own two feet and hustle for what I wanted. If I was ever in any serious trouble, my Pop Pop would bail me out, but there he was lifeless in front of me. I had no bailout plan and it never became more real than when I returned back to school.

    I returned to LA with even more determination to succeed and more selfishness. Whatever I wanted, I was going to have to go for full throttle. There were no more safety nets. I would have to challenge myself in ways unimaginable. To begin, the end of the 4th semester was coming to a close and it was time for payment for the following semester. My financial aid package wasn't enough to cover my tuition. I was about $13,000 short and only making about $300 per week. As the payment deadline approached I scrambled to discover ways to make the numbers make sense. I opted to cancel my housing to eliminate $11,000 from my tuition. It just so happened that a co-worker of mine at the time had decided to move to Las Vegas, creating a vacancy in his North Hollywood apartment. I jumped at the opportunity. The rent was barely affordable, but I was accustomed to living beneath my means during my time in New York. I was still $2000 short of my costs to attend the 5th semester. I was determined to continue my education.

I could not stop again. I already left two colleges prior with partial completion. I remembered feeling unaccomplished as my life became working to pay bills. This was not going to happen to me again. I reached out to my dad to ask him for money but he was unable to help in the way I needed, which further perpetuated my negative beliefs about him. I repeatedly asked the school if any grants or scholarships were available to me. They suggested I take a break. They didn't understand, I couldn't afford to take a break. I couldn't tell my family that I was out here unable to afford school after they supported me and shipped me off. I told them I would work on getting the money.

I went to work determined to make my tips add up, but night after night I returned disappointed by my customers or upset at my boss for scheduling me for an unprofitable shift. I began to resent my job. All of my co-workers hated it as well. The environment was toxic and our performances were being unfairly judged by kiosks at a table. The atmosphere made it hard to properly serve customers with a smile, knowing the money and stress would not be worth it. Yet, none of us left. I would smoke half a blunt faithfully to prepare for my shift, saving the other half to deal with the stress of the day. This became my routine. I vlogged about how much I hated the job for a series of months. I was dealing with a racist boss, rude customers, and work drama just to make a few dollars that barely added to my " keep Asia in school" fund.

As weeks dwindled to days, I began to feel defeated with the deadline approaching. I had to deal with the embarrassment and disappointment of taking yet another break from school unsure of what I was going to do. One night of being high, I had a revelation. I decided that I would still continue to challenge myself in artistic ways. There was no way that I would waste my time feeling sorry for myself. After all, I was still living in LA, with knowledge and skills that I didn't have before. I wouldn't allow myself to become lazy, so I created a full schedule. I signed up for multiple dance classes, made a workout regimen and decided I would use this time to invest in studio time for my music. I began to feel like I was going to be ok. Success would be mine no matter what! One day, an email from FAFSA came letting me know that funds would be disbursed for the upcoming semester. I rushed down to AMDA's financial aid office to officially withdraw before any money was spent. It was the first day of classes. Seeing all of the excited students comparing their schedules and smiling on the piazza saddened me as I made my way to the Tower building. I sat in the lobby waiting for my name to be called. When it was, I headed to the office, sat down, and let the assistant know I was officially withdrawing. As we reviewed my file, her eyebrow raised. She seemed to notice something that wasn't there before. My account hadn't been updated since canceling my housing so it didn't reflect a $2000 balance. We were able to work out a monthly payment after the corrected adjustments. She pulled up my transcripts from my previous schools and showed me that I was ahead in my curriculum and that I was exempt from retaking courses. I was able to fill up my schedule with electives such as dance and singing. I walked into the office prepared to withdraw and walked out with a full schedule and attended class that night. I was sooooo hype!

    I also signed up to audition for all of the school's productions, both musical and acting. I felt unstoppable and victorious going into them after leaving the office with a full roster. The following week callbacks went up, and I was called back for every production that I auditioned for. It felt like I was finally winning, like all of the sacrifices weren't in vain, and I was finally being recognized for my talents. I ended up accepting two roles, both acting. These productions would cause me to be in rehearsals from 7 p.m.-11 p.m. for the entire semester on top of the 15 credits I was taking. These rehearsals would also cause me to cut hours at work, but I figured I would be able to handle everything. I was accustomed to spreading myself too thin. I felt like Superwoman, able to accomplish any and every task with excellence and precision. The problem with piling your plate up high is that you never get to execute at peak performance. One area has to suffer. My finances were the first thing to suffer. Basic math told me that I would have a decrease in my income. I was hoping that my boss would understand my new accomplishments and work with me to schedule me on the weekends. He however, was less than excited when I let him know that due to productions, I would no longer be able to work during the week. Instead of being helpful, like my previous boss in New Jersey, he punished me and altered my schedule in a way that would encourage me to quit my roles and desire to work more. I really felt like he was a hater! He knew that the majority of his staff were artists and that our work there was just to survive. Why wouldn't he be more understanding? He was being selfish, but so was I. I didn't really care about how altering my weekly schedule would change the dynamic in his business. All I cared about was being seen. I worked my behind off for four semesters and was finally going to be able to showcase my talent to AMDA's community.

My new work schedule drastically decreased my funds and made it difficult to afford rent. I was very prideful and wouldn't dare ask for help. I was going to have to figure it out. It wasn't much to figure out. I simply was not able to afford the cost of living, working two patio shifts a week. I became offended when my roommate inquired about rent. She saw what crappy shifts I was working. Couldn't she understand that I was doing the best that I could with my load? She did understand, but she also understood the correlation between late fees and credit scores. She was a hustler who took pride in her healthy financial habits and excellent credit. She constantly begged me to be honest with her about my finances, so that she could make necessary actions to pay my part until I was able. Pride made me feel belittled and attacked, but I decided that she was right, and my pride would have to be put to the side. I would have to ask for her help, even if that meant me owing her. For months, I played catchup, paying her back month after month because my job was not substantial. This killed my pride. I eventually began to take control of my finances and made cuts where necessary so that I could afford my bills. My efforts were met with difficulty as my car was towed for registration. I felt like I couldn't catch a break. It wasn't that I didn't want to register my car, I couldn't afford it. I also couldn't afford the daily holding costs compiled at the tow yard. I decided to reach out to my Mom Mom and ask for help. She was able to contribute to the "get Macy out of jail" fund. It was a few weeks before my 25th birthday when the pieces of my life seemed to be falling into place, and then they began to erode as quickly as they melded.

One of my roommates worked a job that barely afforded him rent (like me), and he became restless of the work to live routine. He let me and my other roommate know that he would be moving to Las Vegas, with our friend who moved prior. I was less than pleased. I immediately went into panic mode as I began thinking about where I would live. I'd already forfeited my housing to be able to afford tuition. I was just getting to a point when I wasn't having to pay back my other roommate every week. Macy had just gotten out of jail and registration fees were in the process of being paid, and here we go! At the time, I also had people coming to visit me for my birthday. It was the absolute worst timing. Didn't he know that I was struggling to stay afloat? He did, but he was worried about his well-being, and so was I. I scrambled to find lodging as our move-out date approached, but I was unsuccessful. One thing that I knew for sure is that I was not about to take a semester break. The semester was halfway through and the stress of juggling school, rehearsals, bills, and moving again began to weigh on me. I longed for my Pop Pop more than ever. I thought about how none of this would be happening if he was here. The fact though, was that he wasn't here. God was, and it was at this point that He began to call me to press into him as He'd done before, multiple times in my life, but I refused Him. I was angry with Him for taking my Pop Pop and angry that He'd allowed me to get to such a low point. I figured I would have to find solutions for my problems because I was alone. 45 became elected during this time and I was reassured that everything was going to hell. Coincidently, Mercury was in retrograde, and multiple people seemed to be living in limbo. (P.S. There is no truth to the correlation of astrology and the path of your life but that's for another book!) I wasn't the only one who life was happening to, but it sure felt like it. I was afraid and alone and on the brink of homelessness, but then a door opened.

Word spread amongst my peers that I needed a place to stay. I was desperate to find a roommate and it just so happened that a vacancy was opening up with one of my hardworking peers from New York on a street named Carlton Way. I was sure that this was a sign. The rent was only $370 in comparison to the $1200 that I was paying for rent and utilities in North Hollywood. I was going to catch a break, until I received news that I wouldn't actually be able to move in for two months until my space became available. What was I going to do until then? Where would I stay? I would stay with my road dog who was down with me since our crucial time in New York, my person, my Dito.

CHAPTER 10

I'm Grown (More Growing to Do)

Before I moved to La, one of my concerns was leaving my "adult" life that I had created in New Jersey to start all over with fresh high school graduates. I'd been living on my own for 5 years, had multiple apartments and a house, attended two colleges, played house in a four-year relationship, and trained bartenders. I was so "grown" in my mind and couldn't believe that I was leaving to dorm with "children". I left with an attitude of arrogance attached to my determination to succeed. I figured that I had an advantage over my peers, and in a way I did. Being "homesick" and dealing with the real world were not unfamiliar facets of life for me. I didn't worry about getting distracted by any boys because they were all the age of my little brother. I figured it would be a cakewalk, and I could play advisor to anyone needing advice. I had the nickname "Mama Asia" amongst my peers for the way that I behaved. I spoke into so many lives and gave my tidbits of wisdom. I felt powerful and important. I loved that I possessed a deeper level of understanding when it came to life and could access emotions from my experiences for my work. My teachers and I were able to connect on concepts of adulthood that I felt my peers could never, due to lack of experience. I felt superior. All of my life I gravitated towards older crowds because I felt like my age group lacked wisdom and maturity. If there was an opportunity for me to gain insight into possibilities of my future, I wanted in; a reason why I was always under my grandmother. Some would describe me as an old soul and I would agree. Wisdom was attractive to me despite my age. There's a calm confidence that comes with it and I was sensitive in noticing it in others. I noticed this calm fire in Dito during a rehearsal in our first semester.

We were assigned to a scene entitled Cry Havoc, where we played nurses during WWII. In the scene, my character was a tough-as-nails kind of girl with a leg injury, and Dito's character was a sweet helpful comrade who looked after me. We always say that this scene foreshadowed our relationship. Dito was the youngest of our class at 17 and small in stature, but I noticed a fire in her during one of our rehearsals. We and our scene partners couldn't agree about one thing or another, and tension began to rise as we each tried to silence each other, and then Dito spoke up. It was very surprising. I don't remember what she said, but it was something along the lines of, "Everyone get yourself together, so that we can figure this scene out". She got us back on track and rehearsal turned out well. In that moment she was able to surpass the petty bickering, command everyone's attention, and remind us of the task at hand while being respectful. I noticed that calm, confident, wisdom and I was attracted to her fire. She reminded me of me in a way. I noticed her fire and I nicknamed her " Spicy Blueberry", due to her fire and her love for blueberries. I knew that from that moment I wanted to take her under my wing to explore her fire. She was special.

Dito and I's relationship became fortified two semesters later during our NYE where we shared a jail cell-sized room. Earlier I spoke about our rigorous curriculum and starving artist lifestyle. We supported each other emotionally, mentally and physically. We worked out together every morning in Central Park before we began our long days, read hours of Shakespeare together, drilled each other on lines, and provided emotional support as we struggled to reach the high standards set up for us, and we did it in excellence! I was so happy that we ended up rooming in our little Strat Hole. Because we shared such close quarters, she was able to get front-row seats to my dysfunction as I tried to hold on to my New Jersey life. She saw all the disappointments and heartbreaks. She witnessed me waking up out of my sleep fighting. With every experience I offered her some insight on how not to accept B.S. from anyone, how to be strong, and how to be independent. I felt like she looked up to me, and I never wanted her to experience the pain that I was feeling. I began explaining to her why I was so sassy/rude and wouldn't take nonsense from anyone. I prided myself on walking in excellence in every area and encouraged her to do the same despite what anyone thought of her. She was a boss and I wanted her to know it. I think like Dito, many of my peers trusted my advice because I was "grown". I thought I was grown too, I really did. What I really was, was broken, confused, and unwilling to appear like I didn't have it all together. I was so stuck on being an example for everyone, that I neglected to do the groundwork necessary for my real growth. Instead, I constantly made excuses for my ignorant approach and justified my actions by naming it wisdom. I believed I was doing the right thing. I believed in people who believed in me. I deemed them dependable, loyal, and worthy of my love. Dito was my person. She saw all the ugly I experienced, understood me, and didn't try to change me. She supported me through all of my shortcomings and she knew she could depend on me to do the same.

When we returned to LA, we continued to be roommates, encouraging each other to strive through difficult scene partners and keep each other inspired when our classes failed to present a challenge. Determined to be snatched, we continued to be workout partners, testing our physical limits with hikes and physical circuit classes. New York made us masters of our scholastic endeavors, but when Mercury's retrograde occurred, both of our lives seemed to turn on their heads. I for one was dealing with financial burden and homelessness while still making it look like I had it altogether. I held my head high as I fearlessly headed into classes and rehearsals, determined to succeed, and at night I humbly crawled into Dito's twin-sized dorm bed as we cuddled to fit. Night after night I was grateful to have somewhere to lay my head, but on the inside, I was ashamed of what my life had become and disappointed in myself for losing control. My big and bold choices had brought me to a place where I had no choice but to be vulnerable, down to the white meat. I felt embarrassed sometimes. I heard whispers in the hallway amongst the other roommates in the bungalow, the same classmates I deemed unfit scene partners and attention whores. In my mind, I was a charity case. Of course it wasn't true, but that's how it felt. Those feelings were magnified when one of the roommates began to spread my business all over campus. Not only was I embarrassed but infuriated. I seriously wanted to fight, and let Dito know that I was ready and willing to punch this girl in her face if she couldn't control her mouth. I was fearful of being put out of school if they'd found out that I was staying on campus for free. I gave every effort I could to strive in class and productions to cover my embarrassment. I never liked asking for help and took pride in being able to stand on my own two feet. I falsely believed that if I couldn't find a way to be successful on my own, that I was weak. I never wanted to have someone help me just to turn around and throw in my face what they'd done for me. My attitude was as long as I'm in control of my choices, I'd be fine. The truth was my choices sometimes led me further and further into a rut and there was nobody to blame but me. I longed to be in control so badly, that I ultimately lost control, not understanding that I didn't have to be. I wish I would have realized at this point, that God was calling me yet again, asking me to lean on Him as my provider and leader of my life because He ordered my steps. It's so funny because it's something I would confess all of the time," MY STEPS ARE ORDERED!" Even when I wasn't looking for God, I always held onto His promises that He made. When I didn't believe in myself, those promises helped me to keep going. When life became painful and unbearable, that single promise reminded me that this was not the end, and I was indeed going to come out on top. This false confidence I worked so hard to build was really rooted in God's promise to me. I believed that I couldn't fall and that nothing could stop me, but somewhere along the way I forgot that it was not by my own doing, but by what He's already done. I thank God for sending Dito my way, because even in the midst of that very low point of my life, He gave me provision. He humbled me to show me that it is indeed ok to ask for help. In fact help is necessary to reach purpose and God will send everyone attached to your purpose into your life at the proper time. I had to be vulnerable and honest and unconcerned about how I looked to other people. No matter how "grown" I thought I was, He showed me that there are always more opportunities for growth, always. He showed me that I didn't have to be perfect, or in control to do what He's called me to do. I can have the true desires of my heart, even if they don't manifest the way that I'd imagined and He'll send help from the unexpected and the unlikely. He used the youngest and quietest person in my class, to break down those walls I fought so hard to build and penetrate my heart, and I'm forever grateful. I love you Dito!

CHAPTER 11

I Like It Like That (Refusing Change)

After a few months, I was able to move into my place on Carlton Way. I felt like I could have things my way too. Things were really starting to look up for your girl. Rent was cheap and I had my own space again. Macy had a parking space in our garage (safe from LAPD). I could walk to school and school was almost over. Dito and I were attached at the hip. Even though I had my own space, there were many nights that I would still crawl into Dito's twin-sized mattress to cuddle. I was accustomed to it. I'd begun writing my first album *Finally Facing Me*, and it was helping me deal with the trauma from my previous romantic relationship. Life was finally at a place where I could manage it, and I seemed to have found some sort of control, but not for long.

Dito began to take a liking to a group of friends who weren't my favorite people. They seemed to be decent people and great students but I couldn't trust them. She spent a lot of time with them and sometimes it felt like she chose them over me. I felt like she was beginning to change and it made me uncomfortable. I also didn't like the bonds that she was creating with some of them. I found myself becoming jealous. Who dares to try and take my Dito?! They weren't with us shooting in the gym! Ok, but seriously, I was uncomfortable with all of the buddy buddy that was happening, especially when drama began to unfold amongst the group. I didn't like how they treated each other in their circle and I was fearful that Dito was going to be a victim of some of that backlash. My jealousy in combination with the desire to protect her made me somewhat of a pitbull. I decided that I would have to get close to these people to see what their motives were, simultaneously attempting to prove to myself that I wasn't jealous, although I definitely was. Upon spending time with them, I found myself actually enjoying their company, although underneath I knew I was always searching for motives. I never wanted to seem controlling so I would advise Dito to enjoy her crew with caution. This was problematic. Although I felt that I had properly assessed the characters of her peers, it was not up to me to project my impressions of them on her. Those friendships would never be able to flourish if there was a touch of pessimism rooted. Her friends didn't like me either. They began accusing me of trying to control her. Dito was in a game of tug of war, and I wasn't going to lose. I was convinced that they did not have her best interest at heart, but I did, at least I thought I did, but in hindsight, I was a problem. When I reflect on my relationships with people I love, I have a tendency of wanting to protect them and going to any length to do so. But how can I protect others if I can't protect myself? It's ok to "look-out" for someone without feeling responsible for them, but I was unable to separate those concepts. I felt responsible for Dito, in the same way I felt responsible for my ex. When in truth it is God and God alone who is responsible for the provision, protection, and healing. Here I was trying to be the god of my life and of others. The arrogance! That was never my intention, but that's what I was doing. I was afraid to lose control.

Dito was my person but she's God's daughter first. I wasn't trying to hear or understand any of that at the time. I was prideful and so I didn't want to play tug of war anymore. I decided to let her experience them for herself without my input, but the seed of negativity had already been sown. Dito knew I loved her, and I would always be there but I was not willing to compete with anyone for a place in her life. Instead of confronting what I was really feeling, I decided to veer over to my pothead community, where we smoked all the problems away. I can't believe how much we smoked. I'm actually curious to know how much weed I've smoked in my life. We smoked every single chance we got, and I mean EVERY chance; before class, after class, on the way to class, after school, before we slept. It was really something. And we were functional! The final semesters of school were too easy, it was ridiculous. It became tiresome. All I wanted to do was get high and graduate so I could go out into the real industry. Ironically my smoking partners were Dito's new roommates. She didn't smoke, so she wasn't with us for a large part of our day. We began spending more time apart, but it didn't stop me from crawling into her bed at night. She had to know that I was going to be there regardless of who came into our lives. I remember her asking me why we smoked so much, and we probably gave off this laundry list of why we engaged, my truth, I liked it. It was something that I could control. It didn't require me to change or grow. It didn't require me to deal with my emotions or frustrations. I didn't have to change, but a change was very necessary for the next level, but I wasn't ready.

I wasn't ready to let Dito go because she made me feel safe. I wasn't ready to deal with my fears because that involved me facing my pain and insecurities. I wasn't ready to lose control of this nice little pace I'd become accustomed to. I wasn't ready, but I wanted to elevate right into stardom. I wanted to skip the process.

Nobody likes the process because it seems painful and long. We have to endure our own process that God has custom-designed for each of us. As long as we fight the process, we will remain stagnant while longing for the level up. You can't operate how you are currently and expect to magically enter the next phase of your life. You will be destroyed in the next level because you refused to let God build you in the season meant to transform you. Sometimes we get angry with God or believe that He has forsaken us because we don't see the promise manifested in the timeline in which we thought it should have transpired. However many of us, like myself, fail to answer God's call and bend to His will. His will is what ultimately transforms and prepares us for the place of promise that we long for. A caterpillar can't turn into a butterfly without going through the transformation that occurs in the cocoon. I wanted so badly to graduate school and land a life-changing role that would propel me to fame, fortune and recognition. I've always known that I was destined for greatness, but I repeatedly fought the process. The process is work. The process is uncomfortable. The process is painful. But the process is also what manifests the promise.

Look at it like this, you can't get natural hair straight without a perm. You can deep condition, blow-dry and flat iron your hair so it appears silky and straight, but as soon as a storm comes and wets your hair, you have an afro again. But if you sit through the process of having your hair relaxed, and clip your ends and train your hair, it will flow! It will be the way you want it. I haven't had my hair relaxed in years because perms damage the hair after a while and most women end up getting tired of the creamy crack and do what they call "the big chop", where all of the processed hair is cut away to let the "new growth" prosper. The hair grows back more thick and healthy than before and you begin to wonder why you wanted to relax your hair in the first place. You end up in love with what you have naturally from the beginning, and you wear your crown with pride. You become fascinated with all of the protective styles and braids and locks that your hair can do. You end up protecting your hair from harmful chemicals and grow patience enough to handle it with care or find someone who knows how to. And this all is part of a process. Sometimes you get tired of the hair when it becomes unmanageable or you get lazy, so you undergo another big chop, free from fear because you know that it will grow back healthier and stronger just as it did before. I didn't mean to go on a tangent about hair, but I've been a self-taught hairdresser since I was 8 years old. This metaphor made sense to me. If I were to treat my life as I did my hair, then I could flourish and so could you, and we will! All of this is to say trust the process and you will grow to love who you are and who you're always becoming.

CHAPTER 12

If God Is Real (Dealing with Loss)

As I write these words, it is in an alley, 20 minutes prior to my 9 a.m. serving shift at Roscoe's. It's the day after father's day and on my bus ride here, I couldn't help but become overwhelmed with emotions as I watched Pastor Sarah Jakes Roberts and her father Bishop T.D. Jakes speak about Daddy issues. I can't stop thinking about my Pop Pop and how much I miss him. You remember the Pop Pop rant in chapter two? I'm still a Pop Pop girl even after his death. And then his death reminded me of my Mom Mom's recent passing, and here comes the lump in my throat that produces unwanted tears. It is at times like this that I find myself questioning God. Why? My grandparents played such influential roles in my life. My Pop Pop was my first love, my first best friend, my first audience, and my first playmate. As my imagination grew, so did his support and provision. My Pop Pop made me feel like I could do ANYTHING that I could put my mind to. I performed my first song written at 11 for him and Mom Mom. I acted out "Little Red Riding Hood" in their living room. I practiced my magic tricks that came packaged in the magic set he bought me when I told him I wanted to be a magician. My Pop Pop gave me an allowance every two weeks for years and made sure to take me out for our own dates and personal time. He made sure to let me know that I was willing and capable to change tires, cut grass with a tractor and fix things around the house. He let me help him make potato salad for Thanksgiving and put my boiled eggs in the slicer for our morning breakfast. I literally can go on and on about the many ways this man shared his love with me. He went out of his way to make me feel seen, heard and important, and for the life of me, I couldn't understand why he had to go in the way he did. God, if you're real, why take him so suddenly? Why leave my Mom Mom alone? And then this year, my Mom Mom passed and this time it wasn't such a shock but the pain was no less gut-wrenching.

After rededicating my life to God at the top of 2020, I was working on an album God downloaded to me when my family group chat asked if anyone heard from my Mom Mom. It was at that moment that God told me that he was calling her home, and I didn't want to believe it. At this point in my life I definitely knew that God was real. I had experienced and recognized the hand of God in my life. In fact, my Mom Mom was my introduction to Christ, the matriarch and prayer warrior of my family. She was my comfort and my prayer closet and the kindest, most resilient person you could ever meet, and here was God telling me that she would no longer be here in the physical. Pain. This hurt, bad. This woman carried my mother who carried me. Her blood is literally running through my veins. Her strength and wisdom live within me and I had to accept God's will for her life, again while I'm away from my family, and I begged God to make this make sense. The pain and anguish that I experienced is something I would not wish on my worst enemy. I have sobbed so deeply and cried out to God when I came to terms with this reality.

Dealing with the loss of a loved one is difficult, honestly one of the hardest things I've experienced. And as I reflect on my life, I see how the pain of losing someone or something that you love hinders you from attaching yourself to anything wholeheartedly because heartbreak hurts-- BAD. I think about the things I've "lost" since saying yes to God and I become afraid sometimes because there seems to be more loss to come. However, perspective is key when you experience loss in life because when you lose, there's something to gain. At the moment of experiencing loss, it's hard to maintain a retrospective lens, but it's necessary to deal with your emotions before returning to the situation. What I feel currently is what most try to run from, the thing I've always tried to avoid, pain! But what happens when pain comes to you? I've lost homes, friends, family, jobs, money, and partners, but thank God I haven't lost my mind or will. In losing, I've gained wisdom, strength, elevated perspective, insight, growth, self-awareness, fortitude and healing. It's interesting how that works. My old methods of dealing with pain as a result of loss have been alcohol, sex, weed, food, work, and anything that served as distraction really. I searched for anything to keep me from facing pain head on, but I had to. It's the brave thing to do. It's where healing starts and your relationship with God is strengthened. I didn't understand that like I do now. Every relationship that I felt like I lost, provided me with provision, protection, validation, discipline, comfort, peace and support, when I'm supposed to look to God to be all of those things. I am thankful that He allowed me to experience real unconditional love on earth, because I now recognize those characteristics in His love. Most importantly, I've learned to value Him and put Him first. When I allow Him to be first in my life, I don't have to search to be validated, seen, loved or heard. When I accept His love, I'm able to love others genuinely and that love comes back to me. That's always been His plan, and when we go against that plan, our worlds may be shaken up to bring us closer to Him. The loss will hurt, but we eventually have to come from a place of gratitude for even being gifted with His wonderful children.

So, yes, you may have to cry. You may have to ask yourself some serious, uncomfortable questions and demand honest answers because that is the way up. It's part of the process I spoke about in the previous chapter, and you'd be wise not to fight it. Stand firm, be bold and face it. That's true liberation when you free yourself from your fears. You were never given a spirit of fear anyway, but of power, love and a sound mind. (2 Timothy 1:7) The more you realize the importance of this, the less unimportant, unworthy thoughts, habits, or fears have room to occupy space and weigh you down. I find that for me, I fight to hold onto certain things because it's familiar. When we practice trauma, fear, addiction, self-hate, and impatience, you become accustomed to its pace. So even when these things bring you pain, it is a pain that is familiar and tolerable. At least if I know what having my heart broken in this fashion feels like, I'll know how to respond. I don't have to open my heart to new heartbreaks. It's like a toxic relationship. You know it's no longer beneficial, but you won't let it go because you've learned to manage it and you're unsure if you're capable of learning how to navigate a new one. The truth is that you do have what it takes, but it requires a restart, reprogramming, relearning, or unlearning and that is frightening. It is the fear of the unknown and that is where faith comes in.

Faith in God. It requires trust. It requires boldness and bravery. It requires your participation. If you're at a place like me, where you feel like life as you know it is shifting and changing and there's nothing you can do, know that it is true and false. Things are changing constantly and there is something you can do. Challenge yourself to change, to learn to grow, and to stretch. Face your fears and let go of everything you can't control and things you are controlling but managing poorly. Give God the reins. If you want to take the next step upward to become who you are destined to be, it is the only way. Just give it up. What do you have to lose?

CHAPTER 13

I'm Taking It To My Grave
(The secret about secrets)

What do you think about when someone asks you," What's your deepest, darkest secret?". Most people probably think about an embarrassing story that happened years ago or the time they kissed someone they weren't supposed to. But what happens when you are actually carrying a deep, dark secret, and the weight of it is heavy? In Black households, there is a saying, "What goes on in this house, stays in this house!". In other words, don't go around telling everybody what's going on. Mind the business that pays you. This may sound wise but this advice is also dangerous. What happens when the "business" is resulting in someone (even you) being harmed. What if your secrets are seeds of destruction that take root and continue to grow with the time that passes? What happens when these secret seeds start to sprout while you are in isolation? What fruits are your secret trees bearing?

Ok, so these are a bunch of cryptic questions, so let's unravel them. Why do we do things in secret? In my experience, when I do something in secret it is because A) I have no business doing it, B) it is not in alignment with the way I present to the world, or C) it is not in alignment with God's standards for my life. All three of these reasons can be encapsulated with one-word SHAME. Shame or guilt is a mighty trick of the enemy which has caused me to claw onto my secrets for dear life. Shame causes you to live in fear of people's opinions and your reputation. It makes you become a hypocrite. You know the "Do as I say, not as I do", type. The mindset of a secret allows you to be unaccountable and feed yourself excuses. You know the excuses too: " Only God can judge me, I'm not hurting anybody, It ain't none of their business, It's only this one time" etc. Secrets keep you from being the real version of yourself.

There are different levels to secrets. There are those secrets from childhood where something may have happened to or by you and only in adulthood have you realized that those instances should have never occurred, and the shame you feel prevents you from speaking out. And because you fail to acknowledge it, it presents itself in other areas of your life. It feels like it's time for an example, I'll go. A deep dark secret of mine is that I encountered multiple sexual encounters before kindergarten. Before the age of 7, I'd seen porn, given and received cunnilings from a girl, french kissed and partially been unclothed by a boy. Do you see what age I said, by 7. Let's travel a few more years. By 11, I'd been molested, molested another person, routinely watch pornography while everyone was asleep, and began self-stimulation. So these are some deep, dark secrets that not even my mother knew about until now, and this is how they transpired in my adult life. During my raging alcoholic days, I would get drunk and make out with my girlfriends. I dabbled with the idea of threesomes while in a committed relationship. I've even slept with a woman and entertained others, knowing that I had no desire for a real romantic relationship with them. This secret seed was planted at 6! Pornography and molestation had a direct impact on the way I sexualized myself and my partners. I was afraid to explore my sexuality with my first boyfriend because I wanted to preserve my purity, but did I already believe I was "dirty"? My perverted mind made me very aggressive and very hypersexual once in a committed relationship. Because of all the years of repetitive pornography and self-stimulation, I constantly felt unfulfilled and disappointed, which made me value my partner less.

Because I had visually experienced countless sexual encounters, it created an appetite in me that wanted sex all of the time, perverted, secret sex. Outside of committed relationships, I was able to take humanity away from my partners and only see them as sexual objects, solely there to please me.

Because I was molested young, it caused me to seek out sexual partners who were slightly younger than I was, just as I was slightly younger than my molester and my victim was slightly younger than me. I always asked myself, "Why are these younger boys attracted to me?", when I should have been asking why I was attracted to them. Secrets. Past secrets will show up in your future in a different form but ring a bell of familiarity, and you mistake it for feeling "right". These are only past secrets that perpetuate secrets in that category. We also have secret practices.

For a while, I smoked weed in private. And when I say in private, I mean away from the presence of my friends and family members who I feared might judge me because of my " good girl" reputation. I knew my mom wouldn't be too happy about it, but in California it was fine. I got over caring and became a proud pothead. The problem with my smoking is I was smoking to numb my thoughts and feelings surrounding loss (which we learned in a previous chapter). Once God gave me revelation about my habits, I stopped, or so I thought. For a while, I was able to be around weed and not be tempted. My appetite was gone. And then other times, I would watch a video of me smoking, or listen to the music I made while high, and part of me missed the familiarity of who I was in those moments, even though I'm evolving. And so, I gave into my curiosities a few times. The first time, my throat became sore, the second time I became paranoid, and the third time, I couldn't swallow for three days. I think it was clear that weed was no longer for me, and yet I tried again.

When transitioning to the next phase of your life, old habits will die hard and fight to be brought along. So the fourth time I gave in, I was high. No side effects, no sore throat, familiarity but a different result. I was not pleased, I felt lazy and unproductive, and I wasted money. In my current phase of life, those things are not cute to me, and yet I was forcing myself to go back to an old thing that caused me to experience negative outcomes. I did it in secret. It's COVID season and my roommate is away, so what better time than now to get "one last time in". I'm not hurting anybody. Nobody has to know. WRONG! God knows, and you know, and y'all both know this ain't part of the plan. What it really boils down to, I didn't want to be accountable or held accountable. My friends would not have judged me if I were to tell them that I'm struggling. I could have easily picked up the phone or prayed, but I wanted to have a secret. I wanted to be fulfilled, even if I didn't enjoy the smoking I was forcing myself to partake in. That sounds like self-sabotage to me. It sounds like a stronghold. It sounds like I needed prayer and deliverance.

What secrets are you keeping and what do the secrets say about you? I find that we don't admit secrets because we are afraid to deal with the reality of who we are, but listen. Our experiences do not equate to who we are. Who God says I am is who I am. That doesn't mean that it's not possible for me to act outside of that. The question is why? When we do things that make us feel shameful, it's important to first dismiss the shame because it is not of God, observe and confess what it is that we are doing, take accountability for our participation, and then repent and ask God to help and heal us. I mean it's part of His duties and he actually desires to, so why are you holding onto your secrets when the truth will set you free?

CHAPTER 14

I Can Breathe Again (Giving it All to God)

It's currently November 3, 2020, ELECTION DAY! If you're reading this then you have more than likely experienced the whirlwind of this year. From COVID-19, to civil unrest and economic crisis, this year proved to be one for the books. I'm sure that like myself, many of you had so many plans and goals set out for 2020. In fact, on New Year's Eve, I wrote out 300 goals that I wanted to accomplish for the year. At the top of 2020, God began to move in my life like never before. I began to hear Him clearly. He began giving me revelation after revelation and suddenly so many things that I pondered and worried over began to make sense. I began to truly exercise patience for the first time. I began listening to people with the intent to understand. I found myself resisting offense and leaning towards prayer. I found myself apologizing to so many people who I've hurt and learning to forgive those who hurt me. I began to breathe again. I learned how to be still and wait! (which is far more difficult than it sounds) I began to learn that I'm not in control and that the plan was never for me to be. As God and I combed over the details of my life in our quiet time, He began to connect the dots that have gotten me to this very moment. He showed me the turns that I made that led me astray. He revealed the enemy's plan to destroy and distract me, but most importantly He showed me how His hand was and is ALWAYS on me. I became overwhelmed by the love, which is ironic because in a way, I was searching for this perfect love that was always available to me. God reassured me, validated me, anointed me, protected me, made provisions for me, and talked to me.

For so long I felt lost and confused simply because I wouldn't give Him what He wanted. What did He want? Me, all of me. I didn't know what that meant at first. It starts at accepting Jesus Christ as your Lord and Savior, but that is just the beginning. This walk is a marathon. It's not a quick fix or insta-solution. Like all relationships, mine with God takes commitment, communication and consistency. It takes love! It takes transparency and having real and honest conversations. It takes letting Him touch those places that hurt. That's when I discovered God is Pain Management. Everything with Him is Good! Because once He touches those dark hurtful places, they don't hurt anymore. He is a miracle-working healer. Yet, He can only heal what you allow him to. I found myself choosing which parts of me I would reveal to Him as if He couldn't handle my hurt. The truth is, I wasn't ready for healing. My hurt had become something that I wanted to manage. The hurt I held were the very links of the chains from which I said I wanted to be free. Oftentimes I prayed to God to break soul ties, help me forget, help me to stop looking in the past, and what I discovered was that it's not part of my past if it still affects me today. Furthermore, those things would continue to be in my forefront if I didn't let God in and touch those places. All the neglect, hurt, and guilt I felt from my romantic relationships continued to manifest in my life from the lack of trust and forgiveness. I wouldn't trust that God could help people to forgive me or that I could forgive myself. I had to realize I wasn't allowing God to be God.

> Forgive: stop feeling angry or resentful toward (someone) for an offense, flaw, or mistake.

God forgave us through Jesus, therefore we should do the same for ourselves and others. When we go against forgiveness, we aren't able to truly accept salvation. That was Jesus' divine purpose here, the reason for his execution. Let His death not be in vain. Debts have been canceled, so why do we keep trying to pay for them? Could you imagine a letter from your student loan office saying that all of the debt has been canceled, but you are still sending monthly payments? It seems crazy, doesn't it? I'm accepting freedom. Here are some practical steps to accepting freedom, Ready:

1. Acknowledge the pain - you can't heal an ailment if you don't admit it hurts.

2. Ask God to come in and touch the pain - God can't and won't fail you. It's in his best interest that we succeed and He already knows what you need.

3. Enter a relationship With God and accept forgiveness- Accept salvation through Jesus Christ. Profess that He is Lord and Savior over your life. Confess that you have sinned and that you believe Jesus has died for your sins. Accept God's grace and mercy on your life. It is your birthright as part of the Kingdom. Claim your inheritance.

4. Accept Peace- Let God's peace that surpasses all understanding heal all the hurt, quiet the storms, and provide proper perspective.

5. Break destructive cycles through deliverance - Break the covenants of demonic oppression that plague your destiny. (We will get into deliverance in another book!)

6. Keep Going! - This is a daily walk. You will not be perfect, and you're not expected to be. Nothing you can do or say can separate you from God's love (and that's Bible!) Romans 8:31-39.

Accepting yourself, your life, your shortcomings, your pain, your disappointments, your losses, salvation, mercy and grace is the KEY to freedom. Don't believe the lies that you have to be bound by your past, people's opinions, shame or guilt. It is an evil lie from the enemy that promotes cycles and stagnation. And as we discussed, stagnation is death! God wants us to continue to grow. He has given each one of us unique gifts and talents to be used for His glory. When we understand that God gives us all, we can shift our focus from ourselves to Him. He owns everything and our jobs are to simply be good stewards over those gifts. AND WE DON'T HAVE TO DO IT ALONE. I cannot stress that part enough. I know that it's counter culture to depend on anything or anyone outside of yourself in order to succeed, but God encourages us to *partner* with Him so that we will see every promise made and every dream come to pass. It is not our business to figure out all of the details. It is our job to accept the call, submit to His will for our lives and love one another. You don't even have to be free from all of your "mess" to do this. If and when you accept Him, not only will He give you instruction, but He will give you desire, but you must first desire to change.

I desired change, real change. I asked myself those questions in the preface and decided, Yes! I am ready. Are you ready?

ABOUT THE AUTHOR

Asia Monae Carlton is a dynamic Kingdom artist born in Chester, PA, gifted in music, writing, acting and directing. She began singing and acting at the tender age of three. In her teenage years, she participated in a mentor group, Team MAC where she created original music and performed it in her community. After studying Music at Essex County College in Newark, NJ, Asia transferred to the American Musical & Dramatic Academy in Los Angeles where she earned her Bachelor of Fine Arts degree in 2018. Asia Monae's art reflects her contrasting lifestyles with & without Christ and encourages her audience to cultivate their own personal relationships with Him. Through her testimony, she aims to help young women heal, understand their purpose, and boldly embrace the divine uniqueness that God has allowed each and every one of them.

www.ingramcontent.com/pod-product-compliance
Lightning Source LLC
Chambersburg PA
CBHW031224090426
42740CB00007B/695